MW00880657

Hope you are enriched

by this "hour" of

cinema studies.

Hope you are enriched by this "how" of Cinema studies.

[signature]

Everything you need to know about

The Films of Sam Mendes

UNDER ONE HOUR

The Directorial Authorship of:

American Beauty - Road to Perdition - Jarhead

Revolutionary Road - Away We Go

Skyfall - Spectre

Written By **Michael Jolls**

COPYRIGHT

The Films of Sam Mendes Under One Hour
By Michael Jolls

Copyright © 2016 Under One Hour, LLC

Published by Under One Hour, LLC 2012-2016

Discover other titles by Under One Hour at www.UnderOneHour.com

This book is available in print at most online retailers.

Createspace Edition, License Notes

This ebook is licensed for your personal enjoyment only. This ebook may not be re-sold or given away to other people. If you would like to share this book with another person, please purchase an additional copy for each recipient. If you're reading this book and did not purchase it, or it was not purchased for your use only, then please return to your favorite ebook retailer and purchase your own copy. Thank you for respecting the hard work of this author.

TABLE OF CONTENTS

Note: Approximate Length in time is determined by
the average US reading speed of 300 words per minutes.

INTRODUCTION

Consider the names Steven Spielberg, Ron Howard, Clint Eastwood, and Martin Scorsese. Each of these immediately recognizable directors spent two decades making big-budget Hollywood movies which brought them widespread recognition. Their films earned them vast critical acclaim before they were granted the Academy Award for Best Director.[i]

Consider also the names Christopher Nolan, Tim Burton, Darren Aronofsky, Nancy Meyers, David Fincher, and Paul Greengrass. At the time of this writing (summer 2016), none of these directors have won an Academy Award for Best Director, or directed a film to have earned Best Picture. Yet each of them has at least a decade of experience under their belt, and each has two blockbusters on their resume.[1][ii]

Now, consider Sam Mendes, Great Britain's wunderkind who throughout the 1990's developed the Donmar Warehouse into one of London's most respectable theatres. He spent over a decade as a stagehand, sweeping floors, coordinating rehearsals, and directing plays before trying his hand at filmmaking. Mendes' theatre reputation landed him a meeting with Steven Spielberg in the late '90s, ushering forward his first movie directing job: *American Beauty* for DreamWorks Studios. The film achieved both blockbuster status and coveted Academy Award wins for Best Director and Best Picture of 1999.

Undoubtedly, the results of the Academy Awards ceremony on March 26th, 2000, has maintained the greatest influence over Mendes' career in movies. In contrast to the directors mentioned previously, Mendes remained a rarity: his very first feature-length movie achieved accolades that some filmmakers would sell their souls for. When asked in interviews about the runaway success of *American Beauty*, Mendes disclosed profound gratitude with an awkward, apologetic undertone for his early, unusual blessings. Occasionally Mendes refers to *American Beauty*'s success as a "bank loan,"[iii] which he would spend the subsequent years trying to justify himself worthy of

---

[1] A general rule of thumb: when a film earns over $100 million dollars at the domestic box-office, it's considered a "blockbuster". This logic remains askew as it ignores inflation, but for the time being we're using $100 million as our marker.

such instant fame. Since 1999, Mendes has consistently made a pointed effort to remain busy and to display wide variety in the projects he undertakes.

Although this book is exclusively devoted to Mendes' film directorial work, to consider all the projects Mendes has co-produced would be overwhelming. In 2003, Mendes and associates began Neal Street Productions which since has showcased 2 television shows, an additional 6 films, and 18 theatre productions! The massive undertakings of *Neal Street Productions* alone validates any questioning if Mendes 1999 Oscar was premature. (Take a look at http://nealstreetproductions.com/ to see for yourself).

When asked by Under One Hour, LLC to contemplate a book-length study on a director's authorship, I was surprised to see that Sam Mendes had remained uncharted territory in film studies literature. Surely after the massive success of *Skyfall*, some academic would have published a volume devoted to Mendes? Each of his films are delicately shot, host power-house acting performances, have moving music and, most impressively, are incredibly diverse in genre. A thorough examination of his artistic contributions seemed overdue.

In Sam Mendes we see a director cursed with a great blessing. While many of his contemporaries spent decades assembling impressive resumes before being handed the Oscar, Mendes has spent his career constructing an assortment of material in attempt to validate himself. Any suspicion that Mendes' success was premature is unwarranted and will be illustrated by an examination of his varied directorial achievements, some proving to be years ahead of their time.

In keeping with the policy of the *Under One Hour* series, the book has been divided into six segments, each requiring approximately 10-minutes of reading time, although more time may be necessary for study. In Part I, we will begin by addressing the recurring motifs seen throughout his work, highlighting them as to enrich the individual study of the films. The subsequent five segments are devoted to the films themselves, beginning with *American Beauty* and what it tells us about the state of the American culture in the late '90's. We'll move chronologically in the third segment to *Road to Perdition* (2002), Mendes' second feature and a graphic novel adaptation. Our fourth segment addresses the exploration of the American soldier in *Jarhead* (2005), arguably Mendes' most impressive directorial shift. The fifth and sixth segments pair up Mendes' most recent films because the movies complement each other as pairs. In fact, *Revolutionary Road* (2008) and *Away We Go* (2009) are flawless companion pieces released a mere six months apart. Together they present perfect contrasting characters, themes, and social commentary. And yet, after all the critical acclaim and awards for his previous films, Mendes challenged his skill set further by taking the reins of the beloved character, James Bond for powerhouse blockbusters *Skyfall* (2012) and *Spectre* (2015), choosing to work from Ian Fleming's fantastic novels to shape the modern 007 image.

Sam Mendes' filmography has been included in the back for reference[2]. For additional insight, a list of interviews with Mendes is included as well. Due to limited space, Mendes' stage and producing efforts are unfortunately not included in this discussion, however it should be noted that just like Mendes' directorial credits, his producing credits are equally diverse in genre.

---

[2] At the time of this writing, it is updated as of fall 2016.

BEFORE WE BEGIN...

This book analyzes the films directed by Sam Mendes. While his stage productions and other produced movies may be referenced, this book was written for a reader familiar with the seven films listed below. Although we'll strive to be as articulate as possible, please be advised that some chapters may be difficult to follow without having seen them, and spoilers are openly discussed. These films are:

American Beauty (1999)
Road to Perdition (2002)
Jarhead (2005)
Revolutionary Road (2008)
Away We Go (2009)
Skyfall (2012)
Spectre (2015)

When discussing the scenes and characters in these films, **I will refer to the <u>actor</u> rather than the character**. For example, with regards to *Skyfall* and *Spectre*, we shall refer to our hero as Daniel Craig, not James Bond.

THE AUTHORSHIP OF SAM MENDES (FIRST 10 MINUTES)

THE AUTEUR THEORY

The **auteur theory** suggests that the director of a film maintains the strongest vision and most authority when telling that story. Film schools will commonly refer to this as **authorship studies**, stating the director holds the dominant creative vision within the framework of a film production. It began as a more European outlook in the late 1950's and was introduced to the American film industry in 1962 by critic Andrew Sarris; prior to the 60's, the director was not given the same recognition as today.

As the concept and recognition of authorship began to spread in the United States in the late 1960's, the director became a more crucial element in attracting audiences. This was particularly the case in the 1970's, as Steven Spielberg, Martin Scorsese, Francis Ford Coppola, Terrence Malick, and Brian De Palma all emerged on the filmmaking scene with films that catapulted them into widespread recognition.[3] An even clearer example of this shift can be seen in Stanley Kubrick, who had been directing since the early 1950's and had

---

[3] Steven Spielberg's *Jaws* (1975); Martin Scorsese's *Mean Streets* (1973) and *Taxi Driver* (1975); Francis Ford Coppola's *The Godfather* (1972); Terrence Malick's *Badlands* (1973) and *Days of Heaven* (1977); and Brian De Palma's *Carrie* (1975).

already completed films that scholars today consider classics.[iv] But by the late 60's, his movies opened with stronger popularity due to his name; Kubrick himself became a reason to go see the films, specifically *2001: A Space Odyssey* (1968) and *A Clockwork Orange* (1971). As the role of the director began to rise in recognition in the 60's and 70's, some actors began to try their hands at directing, including Woody Allen, Clint Eastwood, Ron Howard, and Sydney Pollack.

The study of a single director's body of work allows the viewer to read in-between the lines and gain a richer subtext of the film(s). Despite how much pull a "name" director has, the size of his or her production, how many theaters the movie gets released in, the rating it gets on Rotten Tomatoes, or who's featured in the cast, etc., the intertextuality can always be analyzed throughout the varied films.

The most common form of authorship is picking out themes seen over and over in a director's body of work. Some examples of this include the superfluous amount of explosions in Michael Bay's films (*Armageddon; Pearl Harbor; Transformers*), or perhaps the long intense monologues from Quentin Tarantino (*Reservoir Dogs; Pulp Fiction; Inglorious Basterds*). Another way of examining film authorship is the way in which a director may remain within a specific genre, such as comedies for Adam McKay (*Anchorman; Step Brothers; The Other Guys*) or the science-fiction realm for the Wachowski siblings (*The Matrix; Cloud Atlas; Jupiter Ascending*). Another way of identifying authorship is by examining how many times a director will work with the same actor. Examples of this are Woody Allen & Diane Keating, or Tim Burton & Johnny Depp.

Within Sam Mendes' directorial features, there are four unique motifs that define his cinema. His films are **character driven**, while brilliantly edited with **reaction shots** to convey an emotional overtone. Throughout the seven films, Mendes has constructed an intricate examination of **masculinity** with his leading characters. However, his most distinct trait is his lack of consistency in subject material, showcasing incredible **variety** within his body of work.

CHARACTER DRIVEN

For the last two decades (arguably three), the **plot** has remained the driving force behind the gargantuan blockbusters. Upon the release of the latest sequel, how many pithy articles are dropped speculating who the villain will be? Or, how often are you told to stay off the internet to avoid spoilers? The constant guessing of which character(s) will be killed off, picking apart miniscule screenshots from the trailer, and even social media favorite "memes" play a role in marketing. This is not a criticism of Hollywood, but rather an observation; movies today seem to require impending twists to keep fans interested.

One of the more obvious takeaways from 'a Sam Mendes film' is the powerful acting performances, specifically that his movies are actor oriented. Even in his debut to the filmmaking industry, coming with a theatre background, Mendes specified his attention to acting craft:

> "I love actors! I have great respect for them. I will go out and find what they need. My language to each of them has to suit their brain. I am not a masterclass director. I am not a teacher. I am a coach. I don't have a methodology. Each actor is different. And on a film set you have to be next to them all, touching them on the shoulder saying, 'I'm with you. I know exactly how you're working. Now try this or that.' "v

The idea of letting a character exist on screen was more common in the cinema of the 1970's. In 2009, while discussing *Away We Go*, Mendes states that *The Last Detail* (1973, Hal Ashby) was the dominant film he studied. Having watched it, "several times, and thought 'It's so simple in its presentation, yet so complex in the way the characters are presented. There's no tying up 'loose ends' and having the characters come back in the end for some kind of payoff. The whole idea of an 'arc' that every character has to have is just absurd. *The Last Detail* presented human encounters as they usually happen in life: you meet someone, you have the encounter, and you move on."vi

Although *Away We Go* was a smaller budget, the notion of character driven films is also present in the large-scale Hollywood productions. For example, the story crux of *Road to Perdition* is a strife between fathers and sons. On the surface it's a gangster film, a revenge tale; it consists of a cat and mouse hunt. However, the overarching theme of the picture rests on the strained relationship between Tom Hanks and his son, played by Tyler Hoechlin. The film devotes a significant amount of time to a father and son developing a relationship that's intentionally absent from the first act of the movie. Mendes chooses Hanks' crisis of fatherhood as the central focus of the film. The theme is perfectly complemented by Daniel Craig and his poor relationship with his father, played by Paul Newman.

The relationship between Sam Mendes and Daniel Craig (they met making *Road to Perdition*) would initiate a friendship that would have major repercussions a decade later for *Skyfall*. Although 007 is a franchise, Mendes was willing to sacrifice a large career opportunity (on a series he loved) by giving an ultimatum to the Bond producers before landing the opportunity to direct *Skyfall*:

> "At the beginning, one of the things I said was, 'If you don't want me to acknowledge Bond's aging, or allow me to do something like killing M [Judi Dench]... if you're not going to let me do that, then get another director.' There would be no point in me doing this, when what got me going was the feeling I could do something new and interesting. To have this hopefully exciting action movie with the underpinning of a meditation on ageing and mortality, loss and parents, and other stuff that interests me and emphasized the thing that Bond has always been light on. He's always been very, very heavy on plot, but he's been very light on story. There is no real story, only plot, and that to me is not a satisfying movie. Character and story are everything. Plot is the mechanics of getting people from A to B, and working out how they meet and how they engage."[vii]

One could conclude that Mendes' character driven motif stems from his decade-plus of experience as a theatre director. "Theatre is not the director's medium. Theatre is the actor's medium and the writer's medium, where I think film is the director's medium."[viii] The large success Mendes achieved at the Donmar Warehouse stands as testament for his devotion to character oriented stories.[4]

THE REACTION SHOT

The opening of *Revolutionary Road* starts us with establishing shots of New York City at night. The camera pans down to an apartment, and *cuts to* the inside crowded gathering. Kate Winslet smokes a cigarette. Leonardo DiCaprio notices her from the other side of the room, and tries to get a better look at this blonde through the crowd. DiCaprio voice over: "So what'da do?"

Cut to, the two in conversation, tucked into a corner. The camera slowly pans toward them. Typical chit-chat ensues, yet after 30 seconds of banter, Winslet poses a serious question: "what are you interested in?" DiCaprio makes a corny response as he takes a step towards Winslet, and sits down next to her. *Cut to* DiCaprio and Winslet slow dancing. Their faces serious. DiCaprio interlocks his fingers with Winslet's, who glances at their hands, and responds by placing her arm behind his shoulder, and then moves her face closer to his.

Cut to a new location, on a close up of DiCaprio's face, sad, scared, and confused. DiCaprio holds the look for no more than a second before he subtly shifts his eyes downward. Suggesting discouragement? Embarrassment? *Cut to* a stage, just as the curtain descends. As it does, a quick *cut to* Winslet on stage, quickly shifting her eyes up, a look of desperation. Or maybe embarrassment as well? *Cuts back* to DiCaprio looking downward suggesting sadness? Behind him, an audience member says, "Thank God's that's over."…. *cut back* to the actors taking a bow on stage… "and she was very disappointing," as the curtain falls

---

[4] Actors who performed on stage at the Donmar Warehouse with Mendes' collaboration prior to *American Beauty* include Alan Cummings, Judi Dench, Nicole Kidman, Helen Mirren, Natasha Richardson, and Mark Rylance.

again while Winslet sadly <u>stares out at the audience</u>. After the curtain falls, we see the actors <u>walk away</u>, leaving Winslet <u>standing alone</u> in front of the drawn curtain.

Inside the auditorium, DiCaprio makes his way against the exiting crowd, when he is stopped by an <u>enthusiastic</u> audience member who compliments him on his wife's performance. DiCaprio <u>smiles</u>, expresses his gratitude, and passes on. We *cut to* a medium-wide shot of Winslet at her dressing room mirror, <u>head downcast</u> and <u>crying into tissues.</u> *Cut to* DiCaprio walking through a crowded backstage, when a woman waves 'hi' to him from across the room. DiCaprio, without saying a word, returns the gesture and <u>shrugs his shoulders</u> in confusion. The woman immediately responds, "she's in there." DiCaprio heads off in that direction.

DiCaprio <u>squeamishly</u> enters the room, then slowly approaching a changing wall <u>whispers</u> his wife's name. A door opens behind him and Winslet appears; both are <u>startled</u> by each other's presence in the room, which leads to an awkward "hi." DiCaprio <u>glances down</u>, as Winslet pauses for a moment, then <u>rushes past</u> DiCaprio to her dressing mirror as she begins to remove her makeup. Winslet <u>looks at</u> DiCaprio in the mirror; *cuts to* DiCaprio <u>smiling and walking towards her</u>; *cut back to* Winslet as DiCaprio <u>places his hand on the back of her neck</u> creating a <u>glimmer of happiness</u> on Winslet's face. The <u>consolation</u> of her husband being there? His gentle touch of her shoulder gives her <u>encouragement</u>? Is he <u>proud</u> of her?

DiCaprio: "Well, I guess it wasn't a triumph or anything was it." As he says these words, Winslet's <u>smile fades to sadness</u>. Her <u>eyes shift away</u> from DiCaprio for a mere second, until she utters, "I guess it wasn't."

The tone of *Revolutionary Road* has been set.

Although the title of the film won't appear for another 5 minutes, Mendes and editor Tariq Anwar **show** the audience exactly what the dynamics are between DiCaprio and Winslet, through facial expressions and body language. Richard Yates' novel, from which the film was adapted, includes the various character's' internal dialogue, which remain difficult to convey in film. Although it's DiCaprio's line that solidifies his chauvinistic persona ("Well, I guess it wasn't a triumph or anything"), the foreshadowing of the events in *Revolutionary Road* are etched on Winslet's facial reactions to DiCaprio.

Mendes' brilliant use of reaction shots is not obvious. Sometimes a director's intricate motifs are pronounced, such as Oliver Stone's political agendas or Terrence Malick's use of theology. However, Mendes' aesthetic of "show, don't tell" is prevalent in each of his seven directorial features. Kate Winslet herself highlights that "It was important to Sam that the story (of *Revolutionary Road*) would largely be told in close-ups, so you could see every single scar, every single mark, every single wrinkle on everyone's face. Particularly, Frank and April. So you don't feel as an audience alienated by that sort of 50's glossy image."[ix]

Since *Road to Perdition* functioned as a character-driven story, with the relationship between father and son taking center stage, the audience is drawn into the narrative by how Tom Hanks reasserts his relationship with his son and surrogate father. Mendes will not allow a solemn Hanks to go into a soliloquy:

> "This is a big disease in films, where the characters try to explain themselves to the audience. It's the difference between dramatizing a situation and explaining a situation. And this movie [*Road to Perdition*] tries to dramatize it, often without words. It was really a question of discussing the history of the characters. When did they meet? Did they come over from Ireland as little boys? Where are Sullivan's [Tom Hanks] real parents, and at what point was he adopted? When was the first time that he killed? Does he remember that? What happened? How has he changed since then? Answering questions is like filling the car with gas. As long as you've got a full tank you can go fast. You need to have information. In that one moment when a character casts a look across a room at another character, it's filled with meaning, and those are the moments that the movie pivots in many cases, not on dialogue."[x]

Each of Mendes' film use the reaction shot in the pivotal moments over and over. Although this litany could be incredibly long, some key moments would be:

- After Chris Cooper attempts to kiss Kevin Spacey in *American Beauty* ("Whoa, whoa, whoa, whoa. I'm sorry. You got the wrong idea.") the camera holds on a close up of Cooper looking depressed and confused after Spacey stops him. The shot holds on Cooper, who then exits the garage, walking out into the rain.

- The death of Paul Newman in *Road to Perdition* is not shown; instead the camera holds on the face of a distraught Tom Hanks as he fires his tommy-gun, pelting his metaphorical father with bullets.

- During a return-home parade at the end of *Jarhead*, a Vietnam-vet jumps on the bus driving the Marines. The vet enthusiastically begins cheering the Marines for a job well done. However, the camera cuts around to various soldiers starring with mixed expressions of awe, sadness, and pity, fearing that they're looking at a future version of themselves.

- Throughout *Revolutionary Road*, Kate Winslet occasionally stares out a large picture window. After giving herself an abortion, and in her final moments on screen, she takes a final look out the window. The audience is left to interpret whether Winslet has found freedom, or if she is still lost.

- *Away We Go* blends drama and comedy, and the tone is perfectly set in the single shot opening. John Krasinski never says the word "pregnant." Instead, Krasinski gives a look of extreme excitement and happiness to Maya Rudolf, who in turn slaps him upside the head, knocking him over.

- Javier Bardem's rage in *Skyfall* is fueled by revenge, but the details are never made explicitly clear. Upon his interrogation by Judi Dench, Bardem removes his fake teeth to show the damage of a hydrogen cyanide pill Dench gave Bardem ("Look upon your work, my Mother").

- In *Spectre*, when Monica Bellucci returns home from her husband's wake, she walks outside to her backyard. A close-up displays her fear, knowing she'll likely die momentarily. The camera holds on her face, anticipating death, yet Daniel Craig shoots the would-be assassins in the background.

The four Daniel Craig Bond films as a group are the easiest display of Mendes' own keen visual style. *Casino Royale* (2006, Martin Campbell) at face-value maintains a "Friday night" and "popcorn" friendly approach, whereas *Quantum of Solace* (2008, Marc Forster) elects an edgy action driven visual aesthetic. *Skyfall* and *Spectre* are clearly in control by an artistic filmmaker with a different scope to them. There are longer, more profound landscape shots with silent screen time of characters simply being present in a location.

MASCULINITY

This motif has become more pronounced with each of the seven films as they've released, with varied depictions of the men placed at the helm of the stories. The theme of masculinity is worthy of its own book due to the amount of material and potential ways to examine cinema's leading men. In each of the seven films, the leading man is pushed to an extent that causes him to snap and fight back.

Certainly fatherhood remains apparent as seen in the relationships between Kevin Spacey and his daughter in *American Beauty*, as well as Tom Hanks and his son in *Road to Perdition*. The prospecting fathers of *Revolutionary Road* and *Away We Go* highlights the fatherhood theme, however the contrasting dynamics of Leonardo DiCaprio and John Krasinski as husbands/lovers is far more telling. Mendes even has fatherhood winked at in *Spectre* to build history for Daniel Craig's relationship with Léa Seydoux.

The physical and emotional strength of the male leads is equally as important to Mendes in constructing the character arches. In *Jarhead*, it's not just the physical heat that Jake Gyllenhaal and the other Marines have to endure, but also coping with being mere pawns in a situation they have no control over. *Jarhead* showcases the results of placing a group of testosterone-hyped young men in the desert with nothing to do. What is their breaking point?

VARIETY

Mendes ability to shift from modern suburbia, to the 1930's depression era, to the Middle East, back into a duo presentation of 1950's and 2000's suburbia, and then undertake an action film is evidence of a man who enjoys mixing up his roster. The pattern is the lack of pattern.

The modern audience identifies many "name" directors by genre. For example, J.J. Abrams has made a name for himself within the science-fiction genre, Zack Snyder with comic book adaptations, or Baz Luhrmann's eccentric period pieces. In all fairness, any Hollywood player can get pigeon-holed, and once they are, it's incredibly difficult to break away from. Consider the director of the crime drama *Mystic River* (2003), the spiritual tear-jerker *Hereafter* (2010), and the musical *Jersey Boys* (2014). Despite the versatility of Clint Eastwood's directing resume, he will always be iconized for the Westerns of the 60's, 70's, and 80's.

Mendes' emphasis on variation was noted by his third film, *Jarhead*. Many critics wondered if it was the conclusion of a pseudo-trilogy on America, but the concept didn't hold much weight. By the time of *Revolutionary Road*, Great Britain's newspaper *The Guardian* found the topic appropriate to highlight:

> "While many of the directors who've influenced Sam Mendes have had a defined style (David Lynch, Stanley Kubrick, and Roman Polanski for instance) - Mendes purposely aims for the kind of career that challenges him in new directions all the time. 'I don't want to be known for one thing,' he explains. 'I don't want to have an adjective based around my name. 'Lynchian', I know what that is, I know what 'Kubrikian' is, and I know what 'Bergmanesque' means. But there isn't going to be - and I don't want there to be - a 'Mendesian.'"[xi]

The task many film critics tackle is finding the intertextuality within an artist's body of work. While some academics may write-off Mendes' themes as "family" or "suburbia", it would be negligence on their part. Grateful for his "bank loan",[xii] Sam Mendes honors it by intentionally constructing an assortment from. The exploration of the varied subjects that Mendes has brought to cinema requires individual discussions of the films themselves.

AMERICAN BEAUTY
(SECOND 10 MINUTES)

It's 1999, the year showbiz will remember for having an onslaught of films that attacked the office cubicle and encourage anti-capitalism. This year, films will rebel against authority. This year will go down in the Hollywood record books for having the most film releases about teenagers than any other year on record. The film to win Best Picture will highlight all these issues.

American Beauty is a story where practically every character introduced to the audience turns out to be a fraud by the finale.[xiii] Kevin Spacey, is a pathetic businessman locked in his own suburban jail. On his last day alive, the audience sees Spacey in total freedom, not letting stress depress him, and doing whatever he wants. Annette Benning maintains the façade of a professional real-estate agent, yet internally is an emotional wreck. Thora Birch, is somewhat introverted, yet by the film's ending has a boyfriend. Wes Bentley moonlights as a drug dealer, yet behaves with more maturity that any other character in *American Beauty*. Chris Cooper is a controlling army colonel, who hates "faggots", yet has buried his own homosexuality with aggressive homophobia. Mena Suvari, in spite of acting out sexually towards guys, eventually confesses that she's a virgin, completely unable to manage her own sexuality.

This is a dark satire that was immediately praised by a vast majority of the audiences who saw it. *American Beauty* earns $130 million in the domestic box office (landing 13th place in highest grossing films in 1999. Internationally, it made an additional $226 million in the foreign box office). The Golden Globes and Academy Awards **both** award *American Beauty* Best Picture of the year. This is the same honor that for the last decade has been bestowed upon grandiose dramas such as *The Silence of the Lambs* (1991, Jonathan Demme); *Unforgiven* (1992, Clint Eastwood); *Schindler's List* (1993, Steven Spielberg); *Braveheart* (1995, Mel Gibson); *The English Patient* (1996, Anthony Minghella); and *Titanic* (1997, James Cameron).

In no way is this meant to degrade *American Beauty,* or suggest that it is somehow weaker for not being a lavish historical drama. Mendes' directorial debut was merely one of many films released in the late 90's that addressed the themes of a **suburban nightmare**, **hatred of corporate America**, and **teenagers**. *American Beauty* was part of this cinematic revolution with a crystal clear agenda: telling corporate America to go fuck itself.

CULTURAL PERSPECTIVE

Why mock suburbia? Why create a satire of the middle-class? Why, on the eve of the new millennium, did Hollywood parade a sarcastic, bitter, and occasionally nihilistic depiction of American culture in theatres across the country? Furthermore, why did audiences embrace it? Why are audiences today still embracing it, often with even more enthusiasm?

While at moments traumatic, the 1990's in America is not considered a decade of massive historical or cultural change as the 1940s and 1960s are viewed (albeit the official end of the Cold War on Christmas Day in 1991).[5] The

---

[5] The Berlin Wall fell in 1989 which began the dismantling of communist Russia; historically the fall of the Berlin Wall is considered the main turning point.

United States did not sustain any widespread cultural revolutions comparable to those seen in previous decades. The '90s were spared an attack such as Pearl Harbor, the event that drew the United States into World War II. The '90s didn't have an intense cultural shift, like the civil rights movement in the 1960's. The bombings and shootings of the '90s were different from the '60's historic high profile assassinations of President John F. Kennedy, Malcolm X, Martin Luther King Jr., and Bobby Kennedy. Yes, the '90s had MTV, but it was not the sexual revolution of the 1960's. The '90s were not the painful Vietnam War-era, with political protests, weighty with the deaths of over 58,000 troops overseas. Although the 90's had a presidential impeachment, it didn't rival the vast conspiracy that shadowed the presidency in mystery as the Watergate scandal did in the early '70s.

For the most part, the '90's in the United States maintained a good economy and wasn't involved in any prolonged war. However, the culture seemed to backlash at a "cookie-cutter" presentation of society. What made Hollywood unleash a series of films with agendas of anti-corporate, anti-office, anti-cubicle, anti-complacent in the late '90's. These films have grown in popularity throughout the 2000's and 2010's, pondering themes we see at work in *American Beauty*.

ESCAPISM AND FABRICATION

There is a wonderful freedom that Kevin Spacey obtains once he blackmails his new boss for a year's salary. He achieves a carefree life, one with enough income to buy his dream car, time to work out, smoke weed, even fry burgers just for fun. Although Spacey's liberation from his **prison-like existence** is the most prominent in *American Beauty*, the theme of 'escape' is not exclusively represented in his character. Annette Bening's extramarital affair enlivens her from a sexless marriage, and her introduction to target practice at a nearby firing range gives her a new form of stress relief. Wes

Bentley's obsession with video-taping "beauty" is a distraction from his domestic troubles.

Are these fleeting characters the kind of people that audiences want to aspire to? The story of *American Beauty* rejects discipline for free flow. The husband and wife live a duality between an ordered life vs. letting beauty flow. Could these characters be accepted by a global audience, not exclusively the United States? Could the storyline of *American Beauty* have taken place in any other country? Mendes advocates that "the film doesn't have a point of view about America. It's a very compassionate film. And it expresses a great deal about people struggling to make sense of their lives in a late 20th century western culture."[xiv]

Consider the collection of films that *American Beauty* is often compared to; they are all stories of lost people trying to find answers in a world they don't understand.

Before 1999, there are two important precursors to consider that display the concept of **violent destruction**. In *Falling Down* (1993, Joel Schumacher) Michael Douglas portrays an unstable and unemployed divorcee who has a mental breakdown wandering through Los Angeles. Although Douglas' crimes are morally reprehensible, the film has tremendous fun letting Douglas expose all the flaws in a society of blind **conformity**. Although compared to Douglas' disturbed and trigger happy character, Spacey will exit *American Beauty* with some salvaged dignity as he stops himself from committing the crime of pedophilia with a 17-year-old girl. Michael Douglas would again star in another film exploring escapism: *The Game* (1997, David Fincher). Douglas portrays a multi-millionaire banker who is dragged from Wall Street and forced to embark on a bizarre quest of self-discovery.

In the very surreal *Being John Malkovich,* (1999, Spike Jonze) a simpleton in a corporate office is given the chance to be famed actor John Malkovich for a 15-minute period. Although, a figure substantially more notable than John Malkovich in 1999 was the cowboy doll, "Woody" in *Toy Story 2,* (1999, John Lasseter). Tom Hanks' popular cowboy would return to the big screen to wrestle emotions of leaving home to **conform** with a new atmosphere where he would be a "collector's item". This rejection of a restrictive life complements Keanu Reeves in *The Matrix* (1999, Lana & Lilly Wachowski) in which Reeves portrays a computer programmer who is abducted from his cubicle to battle crime in alternate dimensions.

We see a trend of **fraudulence** addressed in these three fictitious 1999 films, *Being John Malkovich*; *Toy Story 2*; and *The Matrix*. There is no scientific explanation ever given for how people are able to experience life as John Malkovich. There is a toy who insists on remaining inside his box and wants nothing to do with children. The alternate dimension of "the matrix" is thought to be fake, except for the privileged few who are allowed to know about its existence and enter it.

While the story of *American Beauty* is fictitious, it refrains from employing fantastical explanations. Yes, Kevin Spacey's lustful dreams of a semi-nude Mena Suvari on a bed of roses are extravagant, but the hallucinations are exclusive to him and are triggered by actual encounters with Mena Suvari: Spacey sees her dance at the basketball game; Suvari gives him flirtatious smiles in his kitchen; Spacey overhears Suvari say she would have sex with him if he lost some weight. Spacey's obsession with the young girl initiates his reawakening, but it's real encounters that reconstruct Spacey. Wes Bentley's character, the new kid living next door, ultimately has the greatest influence on Spacey's trajectory, by showing him the possibility of a better life--one free of corporate control. As soon as Spacey gets a small taste of how much better his life could be if he reasserted his dominance, he stops at nothing to break free of his prison-like existence.

At the start of this transformation, during another of Spacey's fantasies of Suvari, Bening catches him masturbating, which quickly leads to a heated discussion of their sexless marriage. However, now that Spacey (Lester) has resolved to improve his life, he is able to finally stand up for himself and not allow Bening (Carolyn) to shift the blame:

CAROLYN

Lester, I refuse to live like this. This is not a marriage.

LESTER

This hasn't been a marriage for years. But you were happy as long as I kept my mouth shut. Well, guess what? I've changed. And the new me whacks off when he feels horny, because you're obviously not going to help me out in that department.

                              CAROLYN
    Oh I see. So you think you're the only one who's sexually
    frustrated?

                              LESTER
    I'm not? Well come on then baby! I'm ready!

                              CAROLYN
                             (furious)
    Don't you mess with me, mister, or I will divorce you
    so fast it'll make your head spin!

                              LESTER
    On what grounds? I'm not a drunk, I don't fuck other
    women, I don't mistreat you, I've never hit you, or even
    tried to touch you since you made it so abundantly clear
    just how unnecessary you consider me to be!

    Carolyn is shocked. Jaw dropped as she sits down in a nearby chair.

                          LESTER (CONT'D)
    But, I did support you while you got your license, and
    some people might think that entitles me to half of
    what's yours. (Pause) So, turn out the lights when you
    come to bed, okay?

   After putting Carolyn/Bening in her place, Mendes allows the audience
to witness a private reaction shot of Lester, smiling victoriously to himself. The
new Lester/Spacey has arrived. Act II of *American Beauty* begins.

ANTI-CONFORMITY AND NIHILISM

   Spacey's decision to reestablish his footing in life leads him towards
social demolition, primarily targeted at his wife and new manager. He refuses
to conform to trivial social expectations and takes on a semi-nihilistic edge

against the culture. Make no mistake, *American Beauty*'s cocky wit and intelligence has remained keen over a decade later. However, what would have surprised anyone in Hollywood, was the warm reception to even more venomous films.

To be fair, the theme of anti-conformity has been utilized in films since the golden era, yet it was particularly prevalent at the end of the 20th century. As noted, the crux of *Toy Story 2* is a form of identity crisis: toy or a collector's item? The plot of the year's biggest blockbuster, *Star Wars Episode I: The Phantom Menace* (1999, George Lucas), begins with a queen who refuses to submit to an unlawful tax code placed on her planet's traded goods.

One could argue that *American Beauty*, while unquestionably dark, doesn't plummet to the same bleak levels shared by the other "cult favorites" to which it is often compared. While Spacey's reconstruction leads him to the very edge of pedophilia, he does not condemn himself to hell, as opposed to a joyfully sadistic Christian Bale in *American Psycho* (2000, Mary Harron). Bale's character partakes in the best of both worlds as he's obsessed with slick suits, shiny business cards, and excess of financial income, yet his escapism is obsessing over his music collection, mauling co-workers, and watching himself have sex with prostitutes before killing them.

The morals of *American Beauty* are debatable, yet Alan Ball's screenplay does not allow his lead character to have intercourse with the young lady, unlike the outcome of the Todd Solondz's *Happiness* (1998). Similar in story structure in its variety of characters, *Happiness* also functions as a kaleidoscope into the American culture in the quest for prosperity, divorce, and sexualizing of underage children. Solondz's perverted screenplay features sexually disturbed men seeking bizarre and unhealthy means of pleasure, with little remorse for their actions.

Yet, it's David Fincher's *Fight Club* (1999) that has become the archetype for corporate capitalistic hatred. Of all the films included in this litany, *Fight Club* celebrates a **cynical outlook** on the modern culture, all while pointing a finger at brand names and ridiculing what viewers hold important in life. Audiences laughed at the cubical satire *Office Space* (1999, Mike Judge) in which an adorable oddball gets so fed up with his employers that he actually sets the building on fire, yet *Fight Club* remains the only film to grant the ultimate satisfaction to its characters by blowing up all the credit card buildings.

Two years before 9/11, Brad Pitt proclaims his actions "The Beginning. Ground Zero".

Fight Club's emphasis in mocking capitalistic consumerism comes from Fincher's years of experience in shooting commercials. This is an example of when a director adds his or her unique touch, similar to the way Sam Mendes (as a Brit) gives an objective point-of-view to suburbia in *American Beauty*. Although Alan Ball's screenplay paints a sinister portrait about the United States, Mendes is able to focus on the characters objectively: "I really do hope it's a very private experience watching the film. It's not a public statement, it's a very private, interior film and much of what is good comes out of moments of solitude, where a character is left alone and you as a viewer can share those moments with the character, and very often those scenes are wordless."[xv]

Spacey's greatest revolt against conformity is seen in one of *American Beauty*'s most heart-breaking scenes, a moment between he and Bening. Despite his previous antics, Spacey/Lester finally appeals to Bening's/Carolyn's sentimental side, seducing her, and encouraging her to find her loss bliss:

LESTER
(sentimentally)
Christ, Carolyn. When did you become so… joyless?

CAROLYN
(taken aback)

Joyless?! I am not joyless! There happens to be a lot about me that you don't know, mister smarty man. There is plenty of joy in my life.

LESTER
(leaning towards her)

Whatever happened to that girl who used to fake seizures at frat parties when she got bored? What who used to run up to the roof of our first apartment building to flash the traffic helicopters? Have you totally forgotten about her? Because I haven't.

His face is close to hers, and suddenly the atmosphere is changed. She pulls back automatically, but it's clear she's drawn to him. He smiles, and moves even closer, holding his beer loosely balanced. Then, just before their lips meet...

                    CAROLYN
    Lester. You're going to spill beer on the couch.

She's immediately sorry she said it, but it's too late, His smile
fades, and the moment is gone.

                    LESTER
    So what? It's just a couch.

                    CAROLYN
                (voice risen)
    This is a four thousand dollar sofa upholstered in
    Italian silk. This is not "just a couch."

                    LESTER
                (yelling)
    It's just a couch! This isn't life. This is just stuff.
    And it's become more important to you than living. Well
    honey, that's just nuts.

Carolyn stares at him, on the verge of tears, then turns and walks
out of the room before he can see her cry.

                    LESTER
                (calling after her)
    I'm only trying to help you.

In a 2015 video interview, David Poland of the *DP/30: The Oral History of Hollywood* YouTube series claims offhandedly that *American Beauty* was "Oscar bait", and Mendes stops him to insist otherwise. Specifically, Mendes points out that the film had no giant movie stars in it, the three adolescent actors were unknown, it had a small budget, and that even the *Los Angeles Times'* Fall Preview failed to mention the movie. This illustrates that *American Beauty* was a relatively modest undertaking and did not present itself as a blockbuster, but rather something more unique. *Office Space; The Matrix;* and *Toy Story 2* are titles that we can easily envision watching amongst an audience, whereas 1999's Best Picture aimed to challenge us on a deeper level. The viewer becomes invested in Spacey, the underdog, but what does the audience make of his vices? Do we try and justify his actions? Does Mena Suvari's age matter if it's consensual?

The 1990's initiated an era where films challenged morals on a more complex level than simply good vs. bad. Human beings by nature display conflicting morals-- this explains why an audience member can't help but admire a charismatic Brad Pitt in *Fight Club*, but also potentially forget that Pitt is, in fact, a terrorist. Mendes argues that the level of human complexity is the main reasons audiences are drawn to *American Beauty*:

> "You know, a lot of times, people have asked me to describe the film, and I have no way to describe the film, and I have no way to describe it as a storyline. The only thing I can say is that you'll go in and think you're watching the movie, but then you forget you're watching a movie because one little thing about yourself gets caught and then you get hooked on it. And instead of identifying with the character, you start battling between the movie and yourself."xvi

HIGH-SCHOOL DRAMA & THE END OF AN ERA

Dramas and comedies centering on high school are practically a genre in and of itself that rose to life in the mid 1970's, and found it stride in the 1980's. However, from the late '90s to the mid 2000's, films that focused on the lives of high schoolers flooded cinemas. It's worth noting that while 1999 has been recognized as a year of attacks on the office cubicle, 18 films addressing high school and teenage life were released that year. That record may never be beaten, and some arguments can be made that the number should be higher.⁶

---

⁶ *10 Things I Hate About You* (1999, Gil Junger); *American Beauty* (1999, Sam Mendes); *American Pie* (1999, Paul Weitz); *But I'm A Cheerleader* (1999, Jamie Babbit); *Can't Hardly Wait* (1999, Harry Elfont & Deborah Kaplan); *Cruel Intentions* (1999, Roger Kumble); *Dick* (1999, Andrew Fleming); *Detroit Rock City* (1999, Adam Rifkin); *Drive Me Crazy* (1999, John Schultz); *Election* (1999, Alexander Payne); *Jawbreaker* (1999, Darren Stein); *Idle Hands* (1999, Rodman Flender); *Never Been Kissed* (1999, Raja Gosnell); *The*

The formula of high school films is very conventional: a student ostracized from his or her peers, intermixed with a story of young love. In the year of so many high school themed movies, it should be no surprise that DreamWorks obtained the rights to a screenplay where teenagers are a significant focus of the story. What does *American Beauty* tell us about the first wave of Gen-Y? What does it have in common with the other trendy teen films?

In *American Beauty* we see two different types of romance on display from the teenagers: one highly sexualized by Mena Suvari and the stories she fabricates, along with the fantasies she inspires; the other a budding romantic relationship between Thora Birch and Wes Bentley. The teenagers of *10 Things I Hate About You*; *American Pie*; and *She's All That* also question the trustworthiness, honor, and intentions of their significant others. The concept of adults having illicit interactions with youth is mocked in both *American Pie* and *Never Been Kissed* which suggests **deception** becoming another theme running through high school films. Is it just coincidental that so many films with teenagers in leading roles were released in 1999? Was this a reflection of the time? Was Hollywood doting on a new generation as we moved into the new millennium?

One tendency in some of Mendes' films is how they can be ahead of their time in various themes. *American Beauty* is one of those films. Although the war on terror would enthrall the 2000's, *American Beauty* touched upon social topics that would linger in the new decade and beyond. The debate over gun-control continues, homosexuality would be more opening embraced, and the drastic increase of security camera would make many worry about their privacy in the post-Snowden era. Months after the release of *American Beauty*, Mendes acknowledged that the film "deals in many of the zeitgeist issues. Yes - it touches on issues like ownership of handguns, and old men and young women, on what's happening in the garage next to you without you really knowing. Homosexuality, the military and all sorts of things floating around, the video camera, and youth expressing themselves through the recording of life rather than the living of life."[xvii]

Rage: Carrie 2 (1999, Katt Shea); *She's All That* (1999, Robert Iscove); *Varsity Blues* (1999, Brain Robbins); and *The Virgin Suicides* (1999, Sofia Coppola).

In the modern era, the films of 1999 hold a unique and iconic existence, time-stamping the mood, and reflecting the social setting of 1990's. In showbiz, luck is often a crucial element to success, and Mendes owes his career to the fortuitous timing of the release of his first film:

> "*American Beauty* was perfectly timed. It was the end of the millennium, there was an obsession about older men and younger women in the era of Clinton and Monica Lewinsky, it was post-Columbine, everyone was obsessed with what weapons were being made next door. And it was pre-9/11. I think if it had been post-9/11 it would have been seen as a very navel-gazing movie, but at the time it was perfect."[xviii]

ROAD TO PERDITION (THIRD 10 MINUTES)

Show business is enveloped with stories of great triumph followed by crushing failure. After *American Beauty*, it wouldn't be impetuous to question whether or not Sam Mendes' overnight success as a filmmaker would amount to more than a one-hit-wonder. Would his cinema ultimately prove to be a letdown? Would Mendes return to theatre? Yet the response to *Road to Perdition* confirmed that Mendes was indeed a power-house player, and one who was here to stay: "After our first meeting with Sam," says producer Dean Zanuck, "we knew he had an extraordinary grasp of the material. He described how he saw the scene where Michael [Tyler Hoechlin] sees his father kill for the first time. He described it to us shot-for-shot, exactly as it is in the film."[xix]

Since the early days of motion pictures, **crime** and the movies have remained an ideal match for each other, especially in the American film tradition. Often inaccurately referred to as the first movie ever, the 12-minute short *The Great Train Robbery* (1903, Edwin S. Porter) was a crime piece about bandits. The image of James Cagney shoving a grapefruit into Mae Clark's face from *The Public Enemy* (1931, William Wellman) has become iconic to gangster movies. The famous line, "I'm going to make him an offer he can't refuse" from *The Godfather* (1972, Francis Ford Coppola) has become infused into the American culture. In recent times, critics and academics have declared Martin

Scorsese's *Goodfellas* (1990) an example of prime American cinema. The gangster film has displayed admirable achievements, as well as sustained its gravity for well over a century, and Sam Mendes contributed to the "criminal" tradition by adding to it one of its most pristine pieces.

As a gangster film, *Road to Perdition* functions off the two key archetype of the genre: **the rise and fall of a criminal** which we see unfold from three characters: Tom Hanks, Paul Newman, and Daniel Craig. The drama centers on two connected **families** trying to protect their lives, public image, and capitalistic interests. These motifs are the primary subjects of all gangster films, both in the U.S. and abroad. As opposed to the faster-paced and frantic style as utilized by Scorsese in *Goodfellas* and *The Departed*, *Road to Perdition* unfolds with an elegant aesthetic by means of rich cinematography, a sensuous musical score, and compelling acting performances. The level of artistry invested into the film make it difficult to be mindful that the story originates from a graphic novel.

THE COMIC BOOK FILM

The term "comic book film" often has an inaccurate connotation. Many assume these movies are primarily superheroes (Superman, Iron Man, The X-Men) and are either unaware of, or don't think to include alternative types of graphic novels in this genre.

The relationship between comic book and visual media, has seen fluctuation between prosperity and failure since the 1940's. The current era of superheroes' seemingly indefinite run at the box-office began on May 3rd, 2002 with the anticipated release of *Spider-Man* (Sam Raimi). The positive critical response and hefty monetary gross of *Spider-Man* marked the beginning of a steady stream of comic book adaptations that would dominate the box-office and mainstream entertainment buzz for well over a decade.[xx] To maintain this streak, the genre would display **innovation** in years to come. The innovation that kept comic book films mainstream was foreshadowed by *Road to Perdition*, which was released the same summer as *Spider-Man*. Medes' sophomore film handles itself with a sophistication not usually seen in a genre of big blockbusters and "popcorn flicks".

Comic book adaptations come with a cultural debate over **reputation vs. variation**. Hollywood producers know there are strong outside expectations when portraying beloved, well-established characters like Spider-Man, so any exploration of those characters must be handled carefully. For example, despite the accomplishments of the sequel *Spider-Man 2* (2004, Sam Raimi), it was the lukewarm reception to the third installment, *Spider-Man 3* (2007, Sam Raimi) that shut down production on a fourth film.[7]

While the books and characters of *Road to Perdition* are nowhere near as popular as Batman, Iron Man, or Spider-Man, that lack of overt popularity allowed Mendes' film to resonate with audiences unfamiliar with the story's roots. There was a similar level of freedom seen in other comic book films of the time, such as *Ghost World* (2001, Terry Zwigoff) and *American Splendor* (2003, Shari Springer Berman & Robert Pulcini); while these films stayed faithful to their source material, they were created with a different purpose: to serve as blunt commentaries on the current American culture. Though superhero-based stories are also often reflective of the culture, they are often constrained by the expectations of their own fan base. As articulated by Dr. Laurence Knapp, professor of a comic-book film class phrases it: "Audiences would freak out if you made them sit through a film where Superman just drank beer and chilled out all day."

Reincarnations of adult comic books did exist, but generally remained acknowledged in their own circles, such as *The Punisher* (2004, Jonathan Hensleigh & Michael France); *Hellboy* (2004, Guillelmor Del Toro); and *Sin City* (2005, Frank Miller & Robert Rodriguez), unable to obtain the wide-spread attention that films would have in later years like *300* (2007, Zack Snyder), *The Dark Knight* (2008, Christopher Nolan), and *Deadpool* (2016, Tim Miller). *Road to Perdition* was a blockbuster in its own right ($104.4 million domestically,

---

[7] Sony Pictures would undergo a reincarnation in 2012 with *The Amazing Spider-Man* (Marc Webb) only to cancel again when the sequel didn't stand up to fan's expectations. Spider-Man was attempted again but as a supporting role in *Captain America: Civil War* (2016, Anthony Russo & Joe Russo).

totaling $181 million worldwide) and its success was an indication that audiences accepted comic book adaptations that strayed from the source material.[8]

THEMES OF THE COMIC BOOK GENRE

Genres are filled with themes that give familiarity to the audience. While it may seem odd to compare Tom Hanks to Captain America, or Paul Newman to the Joker, a handful of paradigms of the comic book film offer a unique way of unpacking *Road to Perdition*.

FATHERHOOD

In some tales, both parents play an important role, but the emphasis on and importance of the paternal figure is coherent. For instance, though Batman witnessed his parents' death, most incarnations choose to have his butler, Alfred, fulfilling a fatherly role as Batman's mentor and guide. The examples are endless: Thor is banished from his realm by his father; Spider-Man's formation stems from the murder of his foster-parent uncle; Superman's biological father instructs him from beyond the grave.

Mendes' films often explore on fatherhood, and previously in *American Beauty* the theme is left at a questionable conclusion. While Kevin Spacey spends the entirety of the movie unable to relate to his daughter, in his final moments Spacey transforms into a genuine 'dad'. His entire demeanor shifts to that of a more paternal figure when realizing the drastic mistake he would make

---

[8] While comic book films would dominate the "popcorn/summer" movie business, others based off of lesser known graphic novel origins were released in the independent film sphere, specifically *Art School Confidential* (2006, Terry Zwigoff) and *Persepolis* (2007, Vincent Paronnaud).

by having sex with Mena Suvari. Spacey's character arc is complete once his priorities are realized.

Road to Perdition addresses fatherhood in a brilliantly compelling arc where Paul Newman's biological son (played by Daniel Craig) is a degenerate thief. Tom Hanks is groomed to be Paul Newman's most trusted confidant, in a way becoming Newman's surrogate son. Mendes emphasizes this at a wake/party in which Newman interacts with Tom Hanks' two sons as if he were their biological grandfather. Later on, Hanks and Newman share a piano duet, in which the tenderness between them is witnessed by everyone in attendance.

Road to Perdition's exploration of fatherhood is two-fold as the drama of the mafia family is complemented by the story of parenthood on the part of Tom Hanks and his son, played by Tyler Hoechlin. The film's opening 20-minutes illustrated a cold distance between father and son (both named 'Michael Sullivan'). Mendes crafts parallels between the two: both are men of few words, they don't dance at the party, they both admit to disliking math. In the second half of the film, Tom Hanks & Tyler Hoechlin story is a bonding tale as the two travel and rob banks along the Midwest together. The father and son are contrasted by Paul Newman & Daniel Craig who are locked up inside with bitterness growing between them.

The irony of the *Road to Perdition* is Tom Hanks' fatherly achievement: that Hoechlin **not** become like him. The finale is not so much about Hanks being killed as it is about Hoechlin **not** firing a gun. Hank's greatest reward at the end of the film is knowing that his son will not follow in his violent footsteps.

PROSOCIAL VS. ANTISOCIAL

There are two types of superheroes: those who are accessible to the public and those who are reclusive. Superman, Iron Man, Spider-Man, and Captain America are very open in their interactions with other characters they meet throughout their adventures. Even Deadpool, who may hide his deformed face, keeps an open dialogue with his readers/viewers.

The antisocial group would be the Hulk, Batman, and Hellboy, who treat society with disdain, or sulk with anger and sadness in private. This is where we find Michael Sullivan (Tom Hanks), a criminal of few words throughout the entirety of *Road to Perdition*. In scenes with his family, there is a palpable coldness. Later in the film, Hoechlin demonstrates a stronger comfort level when speaking with his father. In the final scene, Hanks appears at a large picture window of the beach house. In the reflection of the window, Hoechlin waves to his father, but Hanks doesn't return the gesture.[9] After obtaining vengeance and arriving to Perdition -- Hanks demeanor remains content; there is no need for fanfare.

POWER/TECHNOLOGY

Whether from another planet (Superman/Thor), the result of a science experiment (Captain America/Spider-Man), or in possession of disposable income (Batman/Iron Man) - there is a superpower that separates these leading characters from the rest.

Road to Perdition showcases its gangsters as businessmen, not rowdy thugs. They have accountants, board-meetings, dress fancy, and maintain a for-profit mentality. Hence, there is a reverence in which Hanks treats his "suit-case"; the box that holds Hanks' tommy-gun; his "technology"; his super power. Whenever Hanks has to go to "work", he takes his suit-case with him. In the film, Hanks is the only one ever shown with the deadly tommy-gun; no one else is privileged with that specific weapon.

If one plays into this logic, Jude Law is the supervillain sent out to battle Hanks with his own unique piece of technology; a camera. The camera is a tool Law uses as a distraction in the diner when he confronts Hanks. Mendes specifically points out that Law "loads" film strip into the small camera, then "locks" it, as if it's his gun. In the finale at the beach house, after shooting Hanks, Law sets up his camera on a tripod to photograph the dying Hanks. Law's camera becomes a sickening taunt, asking the suffering Hanks to "smile".[xxi]

---

[9] Specifically, in the film's audio commentary by Sam Mendes, Tyler Hoechlin is waving farewell to his father in the reflection of the large picture window, just as Jude Law shoots Tom Hanks.

RELIGION

Some comic books choose to explore the theme of religion, such as *Hellboy* who is the son of Satan, and *The Crow* (1994, Alex Proyas) which portrays the character going through a Jesus-like resurrection. Other films leave religion to linger in the background, as with *Batman v. Superman: Dawn of Justice* (2016, Zack Snyder) in which the society debates whether or not Superman is a god.

Road to Perdition chooses to let religion remain a backdrop of the story--we see an occasional rosary or cross on the wall, as the family comes from Irish-Catholic heritage. Mendes makes deliberate use of a basket of statutes of the Blessed Mother in the countryside church. Hanks prays in front of a vigil of candles while Hoechlin reaches into box of 3-inch tall Madonnas. He then takes one, as if reaching out to a maternal figure in his confusion.[xxii]

The most profound usage of religion is displayed in the final act of the film, when Newman receives Holy Communion (a practice that Catholics insist only be for the pure of spirit) before being confronted by Hanks. They descend to the basement of the church to settle difference and the conversation turn into a theological debate about damnation. John Rooney, the head of the mafia family played by Paul Newman, having already accepted his dark fate, acknowledging that his corrupt son Connor (Daniel Craig) has betrayed him, chooses to do nothing; Newman/Rooney turns a blind eye to the conspiracy and does not give Hanks/Sullivan freedom to murder his son:

SULLIVAN

Think. Think now. They're protecting him now, but when you're gone, they're not going to need him anymore. This ends with Connor dead no matter.

ROONEY

That may be. But you are asking me to give you the key to his room so you can walk in, put a gun to his head and pull the trigger, and I can't do that.

SULLIVAN
(desperate)

He murdered Annie and Peter.

ROONEY

There are only murderers in this room! Michael, open your eyes! This is the life we chose, the life we lead, and there is only one guarantee: none of us will see Heaven.

SULLIVAN

Michael could.

ROONEY

Then do everything that you can to see that that happens. Leave, I'm beggin ya. It's the only way.

SULLIVAN

And if I go?

ROONEY

Then, I will mourn the son I lost.

Paul Newman's message to Tom Hanks, his surrogate son, is to encourage him is to not let his biological son, Tyler Hoechlin, follow them down the same destructive path. Paul Newman has accepted the fate of his death and damnation, yet his resolution is on placing the youth on a path of righteousness.

SIDEKICK

While the "dynamic duo" of Batman and Robin is likely the most popular and widely-recognized example of a hero-sidekick relationship, this concept is more present than one may realize at first. A sidekick doesn't necessarily have to be one person either: Peyton Reed's 2015 film, *Ant-Man* enlists the help of his former crime buddies, or how *Iron Man* (2008, Jon Favreau) is practically helpless without a computer operating system inside the metal suit.

As part of child/parent bonding, Hanks eventually enlists the help of Tyler Hoechlin, who fulfills the sidekick archetype perfectly. Due to his age and lack of experience, Hoechlin is nowhere as experienced as Hanks (nor does Hanks ever want him to be). However if Hanks wants to successfully avenge his wife's murder, and ultimately protect Hoechlin, he trains his son to be his partner in crime. While robbing the banks, Hoechlin waits outside in the car (which he must learn to drive) and learns to becomes Hanks' getaway.

Superheroes' nemeses are generally split into two categories: doppelgangers or representations of what's wrong in society. Batman and the Joker for instance, are considered perfect doppelgangers: The Joker acts without reason, mockingly laughs, and is the protagonist to Batman's grim and practical behavior. The majority of Batman's enemies are extensions of himself, yet within the same series, a villain like Mr. Freeze represents the danger merited by the injustice of big-business.

Road to Perdition displays both of these categories as Hanks' journey is ultimately a personal struggle with fatherhood. Until the finale in the church basement, Hanks refuses to let Newman be his enemy; Hanks' target is his pseudo half-brother, Daniel Craig, who murdered his wife and child. The motive is personal. Yet on the other hand, Paul Newman, Daniel Craig, and Tom Hanks are part of a mafia family, on that controlled society in the early 1930's.[xxiii]

Jude Law as the hired assassin can be viewed as a doppelganger to Hanks' character, in that Law is a professional equal to Hanks. When Law approaches Hanks in the diner, Hanks is instantly aware that Law should not be there. Perhaps Hanks recognizes the traits of a fellow assassin? Law is initially hired help to track down Hanks, yet his pursuit of Hanks turns into a personal vendetta after having the glass lamp shot into his face and deforming him.

COMPOSER THOMAS NEWMAN

For the score of *Road to Perdition*, Mendes would enlist the composer from *American Beauty* for another somber, yet more dramatic soundtrack. Music often becomes emblematic of a director's work over the course of several films, even with a variation in composers. On average, a combination of three or four different composers are often credited throughout an auteur's resume, but there are some cases in which the director and composer remain devoted to one another, as is the case with Sam Mendes and Thomas Newman.[10]

With the exception of *Away We Go*, (that soundtrack is made up of songs from singer/songwriter Alexi Murdoch) the rest of Mendes' films have all been scored by Thomas Newman. A descendant of Hollywood royalty, his father, Alfred Newman, spent over 40 years in Hollywood working as a composer, but passed away when Thomas was only 14. Newman's extended family (siblings and cousins) includes multiple musicians; their combined credits adds up to over 100 films.

The recognizable sound of Thomas Newman's eerie tone, trickled with piano accents many dramas remarkably well. Newman, like Mendes, is unafraid of change; before the two would collaborate Newman expressed: "I don't want to repeat myself. It's a bad situation that way because all of us who are creative want to open different creative doors and sometimes we can and sometimes we can't."[xxiv] Newman exhibits a clear understanding of his role in filmmaking: one in service of the director.

Prior to their first collaboration on *American Beauty*, Newman had dozens of scores under his belt, as well as three Oscar nominations for *Little Women* (1994, Gillian Armstrong); *The Shawshank Redemption* (1994, Frank Darabont); and *Unstrung Heroes* (1996, Diane Keaton). A fourth nomination would be added for his rhythmic characterization of suburbia in *American Beauty*. The most popular track, "Any Other Name," (often referred to as the 'Plastic Bag Theme') some consider Newman's masterpiece. On the films he scored, Newman credits objects and settings: "I start with color, I think about the colors associated with the film and then the harmonic vocabulary so the composition. I don't have rules in terms of process because you want to keep having ideas, and having any kind of rules associated with a creative process is not a good thing. As I say, it is all about how the music fits with the image on screen and I try to write in a passive way. By that, I mean I ask myself does the music work with what I'm seeing, do I like it? If I'm seeing it and the soundtrack

---

[10] Other examples of this devotion between director and composer would be Darren Aronofsky & Clint Mansell, Brad Bird & Michael Giacchino, Tim Burton & Danny Elfman, Sergio Leone & Ennio Morricone, Steven Spielberg & John Williams, and Robert Zemeckis & Alan Silvestri.

is working then I keep going. I try to be whimsical in my approach. I try to be fluid. I sit at the piano and just see what happens really."[xxv]

For *Road to Perdition,* Newman experimented with Irish folk music, adding in his trademark sounds, both dramatic and playful, to create a score suited for a grand gangster picture. He would incorporate a level of heaviness, while accenting the emotional drama into all the scores on which he and Mendes collaborated. "He [Mendes] is so smart. He is so switched on and has great ideas and most of what he says makes sense! We do have a great working relationship and that means that he is very comfortable telling if something doesn't work, he is very much a leader and he does reject ideas as much as he accepts them and I think that is really important."[xxvi]

Both composer and director would take a vastly stark departure from their comfort zones on their journey into the Middle East.

JARHEAD
(FOURTH 10 MINUTES)

In 2010, anyone questioning Sam Mendes as an odd hire for director of a Bond film failed to recall *Jarhead*. Of his seven directorial efforts, *Jarhead* remains the most unique as being the only non-fiction entry and a commentary on the United States' prolonged struggle in the Middle East through the plight of a Marine platoon. As previously discussed, audiences tend to associate directors with genres, and occasionally these artists will depart from their preferred subject material to explore new grounds. Ron Howard has proven that he can dabble in light-hearted comedies (*Night Shift*; *Splash*; *How the Grinch Stole Christmas*), but also masterfully handle historical dramas (*Apollo 13*; *A Beautiful Mind*; *Cinderella Man*; *Rush*).

At the same time, there are other directors who have moved out of their comfort zones and found the departure displeasing. Brian De Palma, an icon in the horror genre (*Carrie*; *Dressed to Kill*; *Body Double*) and gangster genre (*Scarface*; *The Untouchables*; *Carlito's Way*) found the experience of doing the studio-financed, sci-fi film *Mission to Mars* (2000) so discouraging, that he moved to France and has kept his productions in Europe ever since.[11] Yet for a

---

[11] De Palma would use American stars in *The Black Dahlia* (2006) and *Passion* (2013), but the productions remained in Europe.

director who thrives on variety, Mendes advocates, "I don't subscribe to the theory that in order to make a film about it you have to have lived it. I mean, obviously, otherwise I'd never have made a gangster movie [*Road to Perdition*], or a war movie [*Jarhead*], or a movie about American suburbia [*American Beauty*] in the first place!"[xxvii]

HISTORICAL SET-UP: OPERATION DESERT STORM

As *Jarhead* is a true story, it's appropriate to be mindful of the history leading to the liberation of Kuwait and the world's outlook on Iraq in the early 1990s.

On July 16th, 1979, **Saddam Hussein** becomes president of Iraq. Within two months, hundreds of Hussein's political adversaries are either shot or gassed and buried in mass graves along Iraq's rural countryside. One year later (September 1980), Iraq attacks Iran, kicking off the Gulf War, which ends in August 1988. The death toll of this eight-year-long war reaches over 1 million. There is no victor, only a stalemate cease-fire.

The Gulf War places Iraq $80 billion dollars in debt ($10 billion of which was borrowed from the wealthy neighboring country of Kuwait). Iraq's spirit is demoralized, and Hussein cannot pay the abundant stipend promised to his soldiers, although Hussein and his family continue to live comfortably.

...Comfortably is an understatement. Throughout the Gulf War, Hussein continued to spend tens of millions of dollars building his marble palaces across the country. The palaces themselves were a symbol of strength, and many were surrounded by lavish water fountains, as water in the desert is a key indicator of wealth. The palaces also help define Hussein's old-fashioned view of power, believing that the world respected brute, unmerciful strength. Hence Hussein's personal disposition was a mixed facade of threats and riches. For example, Hussein owned more than 200 tailored suits including various costumes for religious celebrations and parties. He reportedly smoked Cuban cigars yet discarded them after only a few puffs.[12]

Hussein appears on the June 4th, 1990 cover of *U.S. News & World Report* with the headline, "The Most Dangerous Man in the World." While the article primarily highlighted Iraq's intentions of obtaining material to build a nuclear bomb, it highlighted much of the same message broadcast to the American people throughout the rest of 1990: "Hussein has already lobbed nerve gas not only at his archenemies in Iran, but at some of his own people." Additionally, "Worse, there is virtually no one, at home or abroad, who can restrain his worst impulses. He has few friends, even in the Arab world, and fewer and fewer within Iraq's own political structure. He has stubbed out rivals, real and imagined, like cigarette butts, and Western intelligence agencies have reported several instances in which he has pulled the trigger himself."[xxviii]

Struggling with the economy, Hussein asks Kuwait to be forgiven of his war debt of $10 billion, but the small country refuses. Hussein then begins a propaganda campaign against Kuwait, suggesting they are stealing oil from Iraq. This eventually builds up to an Iraqi invasion on August 2nd, 1990. The small Kuwaiti forces fall within a single day. United States President, George H.W. Bush, compares Hussein to Adolf Hitler, proclaiming: "As was the case in the 1930s, we see in Saddam Hussein an aggressive dictator threatening his neighbors."

On August 7th, 1990, five days after the invasion, President Bush begins **Operation Desert Shield**, in which U.S. troops (including Anthony Swofford, the author of *Jarhead*) are deployed to the neighboring country, Saudi Arabia. Over the next five months, 32 countries join a coalition force pleading Iraq to remove themselves from Kuwait. Finally, on January 17th, 1991, **Operation Desert Storm** begins with a destructive air-bombing campaign that wipes out the majority of Iraq's air force. On February 28th, 1991, Hussein ends the war,

---

[12] Hussein's eldest son, Uday, remains an even better example of this dual perception of wealth and fear that carried throughout Iraq. Uday owned over 100 luxury cars (200 according to some sources) that he drove through the streets of Baghdad picking up women, occasionally underage girls. Uday was a frequent partier and heavy drinker; in one case, he publicly murdered one of his father's friends at a party. In the mid-1980s, Uday was placed in charge of the Iraqi Olympic Committee and tortured athletes who failed to win. Some torture sessions were recorded for Uday's private video collection.

ordering his troops to leave Kuwait, yet upon retreat instructs them to set Kuwait's oil fields on fire.

BOOK VS. FILM

Anthony Swofford's memoir consistently shifts between an array of stories and locations, from boot camp to summers back home to the years after Desert Storm. "You really are marked" Swofford said when doing press for the film in 2005; "You're changed for life. And I don't think a lot of war stories and movies tell that. They're more interested in battles and soldiers getting their legs blown off or getting blinded by fire. I'm more interested in the personal side of it."[xxix]

Is Swofford's statement accurate? That war movies are more concerned with exploiting violence than trying to tap into the individual human condition? In Swofford's memoir, as well as the film, the soldiers are shown absorbing *Apocalypse Now* (1979, Francis Ford Coppola) and *The Deer Hunter* (1978, Michael Cimino) to rev up their emotions. Are these Vietnam War films ignorant of the soldier's plight? Does the value of these films decrease because they are fictional stories?

Jarhead was released in November 2005, a time when audiences didn't want to see it. The topics of terrorism, Afghanistan, and Iraq were absent from cinemas in the immediate post-9/11 world.[13] It wasn't until the late-2000s that the **war-on-terror genre** became seasonal Oscar-bait. Yet these films were met

---

[13] There are two exceptions: *Black Hawk Down* (2001, Ridley Scott) was released four months after 9/11 in the height of the Christmas/awards season. It was met with positive reviews and managed to pull in $108.6 million in the domestic box office, but it would be the last studio depiction of Middle-Eastern war until *Jarhead* in 2005. Also, while a handful of documentaries were released, none were as controversial as *Fahrenheit 9/11* (2004, Michael Moore) which won the Palme d'Or at the Cannes Film Festival and became the highest grossing documentary of all time with $119 million in the domestic box office.

with a wide assortment of reviews and performed poorly at the box office, as did *Jarhead*.xxx It was not until the early 2010s that a massive shift in the genre occurred, and war-on-terror films spiked at the box office. The new wave of movies seen in the early 2010s were based off of true stories and centered on actual people, such as the CIA-agents in *Zero Dark Thirty* (2012, Kathryn Bigelow) and the Navy SEALS in *Lone Survivor* (2013, Peter Berg).xxxi This raises the question, would *Jarhead* have gained more popularity if it were released 10 years later, in 2015 instead of 2005?

THREE-ACT STORY

The emotions and visual aesthetic of *Jarhead* are so intense that it will (and should) overwhelm the viewer. The easiest way of digesting the film is to divide *Jarhead* into three acts: **boot camp**, **waiting**, and an allegory of **Dante's Inferno**.

BOOT CAMP

The most famous cinematic depiction of boot camp has remained *Full Metal Jacket* (1987, Stanley Kubrick), and army-themed films are very conscious that shooting a military barrack will immediately recall comparisons to Kubrick's film. Nonetheless, screenwriter William Broyles Jr. chooses to integrate boot camp into the story as a viable element of the film. Although the very first moments of *Jarhead* do visually look akin to the barracks from *Full Metal Jacket*, the rest of the sequence functions with the intention of processing Jake Gyllenhaal as if he were an object on an assembly line. Within the opening 10 minutes, Gyllenhaal is slapped upside the head repeatedly by a GI, has his head smashed into a chalk board, is wrestled to the ground, tied up, and passes out due to shock. Even when Gyllenhaal tries to fake poor health by taking laxatives and hiding in the bathroom, Jamie Foxx (metaphorically) tosses him right back onto the assembly line. Mendes uses the Bobby McFerrin song "Don't Worry, Be Happy" as a soundtrack for part of the sequence to mock to how terribly the Marines get treated.[xxxii]

It's important to note that Broyles' screenplay is an adaptation of a sporadic memoir (Anthony Swofford constantly jumps from boot camp, to home, to post-war, to childhood), yet the film is relatively faithful to the book. There are stories Broyles leaves out, and some are added--one being a death during a "live fire exercise", when soldiers are instructed to crawl under barbed wire while live rounds are shot above them (to prepare them for the shock of having bullets fly by). In the column next to Gyllenhaal, the intensity of the noise sends one man into panic, and he jumps up, only to get gunned down. While this scene was something the actual Anthony Swofford did not witness, these unfortunate events do happen, and Broyles uses it to highlight early in *Jarhead* that what the Marines are doing is a matter of life or death.

WAITING

Very few films are able to avoid dullness when a significant amount of the story has characters in a stagnant position. This may be Jarhead's most praisable achievement in that it's a riveting movie, all while remaining in the desert. This concept leads to why Mendes choose to direct the picture:

> "It is odd to play the game with an audience of, well, they're going to war, the war's going to be big, it's going to be huge, and then you train the men to go to war... and then they take the war away. What happens? They create their own war, they create their own mini-wars within that situation, and there's a sort of sense in which the middle part of the film is just waiting."[xxxiii]

There is also sarcasm to consider, in that these soldiers could be mindful of the historical events unfolding, but as Peter Sarsgaard says: "Fuck politics"; few pay credence to the politics that sent them there. Rather, during this waiting period, Gyllenhaal becomes more and more isolated from his platoon. Descending into trepidation of what his girlfriend is doing back home. In a very short, yet poignant scene, Gyllenhaal and Sarsgaard are finishing lunch;

Gyllenhaal gloomily asks: "I wonder what she's doing right now?" and Sarsgaard responds, "There's no way to know," walking away from the table. The scene is brightly lit, wood scraps are scattered on the table, and Gyllenhaal sits, isolated in the hot desert.

Desert. Dryness. Sand. These are the images that dominate a significant amount of *Jarhead*'s second act. The sand (metaphorically) seeps into Gyllenhaal: in a dream he wanders into the bathroom to wash his face, but thinking of his girlfriend, he vomits sand into the sink (in the book it's glass). As Gyllenhaal's distrust in her deepens, his frustration grows: he's unable to masturbate to images of her -- he is drained dry. At a Christmas party, Gyllenhaal goes out of his way to bring alcohol to the party, a beverage that ultimately dehydrates.

As seen by the character-driven motif, Mendes presents a film where the characters purely exist. They have no control on the invasion date. They cannot leave. They have no choice in their friends.

DANTE'S INFERNO

The *Divine Comedy* trilogy by Dante Alighieri is a first-person narrative about a man being given a tour of Hell, Purgatory, and Heaven. The allusions to book one, *Inferno,* are intentional, and are winked at throughout *Jarhead* before becoming the template for the final third Act. Dante's trilogy is smart in its presentation of punishment and repentances. The books are not a litany of graphic depictions; rather each form of torture has its own unique psychological impact.

For Act two, the "waiting" period, we notice that once Gyllenhaal is in Saudi Arabia, his suffering isn't necessarily physical. Rather, his spirit is repeatedly beaten, which encourages Gyllenhaal's dishonorable behavior. He wants to replay a vengeful sex tape sent to another Marine by his unfaithful wife (after it embarrassingly plays in front of a dozen soldiers). The desire to continue the public humiliation is immoral, whereas sneaking alcohol into a Christmas party is merely against the rules. Nonetheless, after being caught with alcohol, Gyllenhaal is ordered to undertake the filthy job of cleaning out the latrines. The words "Abandon all hope, ye who enter here" is scrawled on one of the receptacles; the same words written above the gates of Hell in *Inferno*.

Dante depicts Hell as having nine separate layers (or "circles," a spiral downwards of nine floors), each with its own unique form of punishment. Each circle gets worse and worse. The final third Act of *Jarhead* can be broken into nine moments that the platoon, and Gyllenhaal specifically, experience until the bitter conclusion of not being allowed to authentically participate in Operation Desert Storm.

1. **Dead-Battery Run:** The transition into Act II begins with a battle scene (Gyllenhaal's voice over: "my combat action has commenced"). As the fighting intensifies, the platoon finds themselves with a dysfunctional radio, and Jamie Foxx sends Gyllenhaal to get a new battery from a supply truck. Gyllenhaal runs along a ridge, explosions going off very close to him before reaching the supply truck to get a battery. Gyllenhaal is handed a battery and runs back to his troop. They discover that he brought them a dead battery, forcing him to repeat the deadly run.

2. **Friendly-Fire:** As the military begins their march into Iraq, the platoons are spread hundreds of yards apart. In the sky, twin-engine wing jets (A-10 Warhogs) fly above, beginning advance bombing. However, they accidentally fire rounds at the U.S. troops. A jeep and a convoy truck a hundred yards off from the platoon gets hit and explodes. The platoon is close enough to witness the destruction in detail and see fellow Americans on fire.

3. **Highway of Death:** The platoon comes upon miles of charred cars stranded in an expressway exiting Kuwait. The sight is shocking, compounded with the mixed emotion realizing that if this bombing didn't happen, many of them would likely have been killed by the exiles.

4. **Corpse Picnic:** While trekking through the highway, the platoon pauses for lunch. Gyllenhaal wanders away from the platoon, over a ridge, where he finds five charred remains sitting in a semi-circle as if they were eating/conversing. Gyllenhaal moves into an open space and takes a seat joining the corpses momentarily before he vomits. When Gyllenhaal returns back to the platoon, Jamie Foxx pulls him aside and asks what he saw. Gyllenhaal responds with "nothing," although it's clear he's lying by his facial reaction. Foxx chooses not to persist further. Whatever Gyllenhaal saw is too horrific to share.

5. **Oil Fields:** as the platoon exits the highway of death and enters onto another open stretch of desert, in the distance, the oil rigs are ignited. Fire begins to shoot out, covering the sky in blackness. It becomes so

bad that the platoon eventually has to stop due to all the raining oil. Earlier in the film, Lucas Black's character advocates that the whole war is centered around the U.S.'s greed for oil; hence, it's fitting that Lucas Black's character is the one to have oil seep into his eyes and painfully burn him.

6. **Desecration of the Corpse:** Of all the characters in *Jarhead*, the grossly immature Marine played by Evan Jones single-handedly causes the most vexation for the other platoon members. Throughout *Jarhead*, Jones remains the unpredictable hot-head who taunts everyone with sexual perversion and off-color behavior. His final scene is appropriately disturbing as he's caught desecrating a corpse found in the desert. Although it's not clear specifically what Jones does to the corpse (he says "check out what I put in his mouth"), the moment harvests anger from Gyllenhaal. Despite the lewd behavior, Jones accents Gyllenhaal's frustration proclaiming "This is war! Have we done anything but walk around in the sand? I didn't kill him - he's dead!"

7. **The Horse:** After Gyllenhaal buries the desecrated corpse, a horse covered in oil wanders out of the fog and stumbles up to him. Gyllenhaal pets the animal, and it saunters off. This is another scene not in the book, yet Mendes specifically includes it as a reminder of the effect that the burning oil fields had on the natural world.

8. **"I Love This Job":** It's appropriate that within the hellfire of Act III, Jamie Foxx continues his role as Gyllenhaal's guiding spirit. Although Foxx is Gyllenhaal's superior sargent, everything Foxx does to him throughout *Jarhead* is for Gyllenhaal's own benefit, especially the negative. Foxx cajoles Gyllenhaal to get him through bootcamp. Foxx punishes him when acting out, instilling discipline. In between the second and third act, Foxx entrusts Gyllenhaal with news of a fellow Marine whose morale has been damaged.

So it's mythologically appropriate that before Gyllenhaal embarks on the ninth most destructive level of hell, that his spiritual guide boosts his morale. As the exhausted Gyllenhaal buries the desecrated corpse, Foxx brings him a water canteen (a reward for a good deed) and tells Gyllenhaal that Evan Jones' behavior for desecrating the corpse is intolerable, and he will be punished. Foxx then opens up to Gyllenhaal in a way he hasn't before, in attempt to give Gyllenhaal a sense of pride for the work they're doing:

                              SGT. SYKES
I could be working with my brother right now. He's got
a drywall business in Compton. Does the inside of office
buildings. You know, the metal studs. I could be his
painter. Said he'd give me that brand new Dodge Ram
Charger. You know, the 318 Magnum? The beast?

Sykes pauses, looking for reassurance from Swoff.

                          SGT. SYKES (CONT'D)
All indoor work, too. Lots of AC. I could sleep with my
wife every night. Fuck her, maybe. Take my kids to school
every morning. And I'd run his crews, too. Probably
increase productivity 40 to 50%. Make $100,000 a year.

Sykes pauses for dramatic effect.

                          SGT. SYKES (CONT'D)
Do you know why I don't?

Swoff says nothing.

                          SGT. SYKES (CONT'D)
Because I love this job. I thank God for every fucking
day that He gives me in Corps. Ooh-rah. I mean, who else
gets a chance to see shit like this?

Sykes and Swoff stare out at the towering flames.

                              SGT. SYKES
You know what I'm saying?

                                SWOFF
Yes, Staff Sergeant.

                              SGT. SYKES
Do you?

The moment concludes in true Sam Mendes fashion: Foxx carefully eyes
Gyllenhaal, and Gyllenhaal returns with a look of slight confusion. The
scene takes on new meaning in hindsight as Gyllenhaal (the "author" of
Jarhead) doesn't yet grasp the purpose of this message. The moment
harkens back to the theme of *American Beauty*: there is beauty
everywhere-- one just needs to stop and look for it. While the burning
of the oil rigs caused incredible environmental and economic damage,

Gyllenhaal and Foxx were privileged to be actual witnesses to one of the great events of the early 1990s.

9. **Hold Your Fire:** the final "layer" is the most crushing blow as it dangles hope in front of the war-craving Marines and takes away their chance for solace. Gyllenhaal and Sarsgaard are given a special sniper assignment to infiltrate a building near an airport and take out as many guards as they can. Up to this point, Gyllenhaal (and technically Sarsgaard) have gone through a physical and mental beating, which again, Mendes focuses so much attention on:

"They're trained and they wait six months and they build themselves up into a frenzy of expectation and then they're always three steps behind where the war is because the war is being fought in the air."[xxxiv]

Upon setting up a perfect shot to execute a guard inside the air tower, they are told to stand down. Sarsgaard pleads, eventually outright begs--the need to at least fire their weapons once is stolen from them as the air force swoops in and destroys the tower. Operation Desert Storm was referred to as the "video game war" as the evening news showed green point-of-view missiles flying into buildings. This is where Mendes shares an important outlook:

"There's a key shot for me, which is of Jake Gyllenhaal's character Swoff, which is based on Tony Swofford observing the wholesale destruction of an airfield towards the end of the movie, through a window, and the look on his face always seems to say: 'I'm never going to be a part of this war, I'm always going to be an observer.' But the irony is that in not fighting, somehow he remains intact--in not getting his kill, in not having blood on his hands when he returns home, he somehow has his own life saved. So there is some kind of redemption."[xxxv]

DESERT STORM IS NOT 2003

Bearing in mind that *Jarhead* was released during the United States' occupation of Iraq, audiences and critics couldn't help but assume the possibility of a subliminal political message. Although earlier drafts of the screenplay included a reference to the 2003 invasion of Iraq in the film's coda, *Jarhead* does not acknowledge the era in which it was released (There is a brief moment of Jamie Foxx leading troops through a war zone, but the location is never specified, so the brief scene is open to interpretation).

Although the temptation was great, Mendes made the superior decision to avoid "tipping the hat" to 2003. The brilliant and sensible choice allows the true characters in *Jarhead* to remain exclusive to their story which is Operation Desert Storm.

> "I'm interested in those personal stories, not taking a political stand," Mendes explains. "I don't think people are battle-fatigued. If anything, they've tuned out to what's happening. I don't know that many people realize what a war does, on the personal scale. Hopefully, this [Jarhead] will get people thinking. That's the best thing a film can do."xxxvi

REVOLUTIONARY ROAD VS. AWAY WE GO (FIFTH 10 MINUTES)

1950s vs. 2000s. Wide release studio budget vs. limited release independent. The lavish upper-middle class Leonardo DiCaprio & Kate Winslet compared to the simplistic low-income John Krasinski & Maya Rudolph. A married couple just turning 30 with two children, in contrast to an unmarried couple rapidly approaching their mid-30s, expecting their first child. One couple longs to escape a counterfeit society; the other couple travels the country to find a home. Regret vs. carefree. Bitterness vs. laughter. Male chauvinism vs. heartfelt tenderness. "Fuck you, you empty hollow shell of a woman" vs. "I will always love you, even if you're enormous."

THE COMPANION PIECE

Film academics often analyze a director's body of work by looking for ways their films "talk" to one another. Sam Mendes' *Revolutionary Road* and

Away We Go fall into the category of **companion piece**. This doesn't mean they are pseudo-sequels, where a handful of characters reappear; rather, companion pieces are two films from the same director, both dramatically different yet intentionally similar. A companion piece film series remains best watched as one single work of art.

Considering that a companion piece requires two separate productions, it's no surprise there aren't more of them. In the case of Clint Eastwood's depiction of the World War II battle of Iwo Jima, *Flags of Our Fathers* and *Letters from Iwo Jima* (2006), both films were produced simultaneously. The films recount stories of young soldiers struggling with higher command and the culture of their home countries. The respective movies articulate the same emotions shared by soldiers on either side of the war. [xxxvii]

When Darren Aronofsky's *The Wrestler* (2008) was released in theaters, the majority of the media buzz centered on Mickey Rourke's powerhouse performance. *The Wrestler* was a stand-alone production; its second half, *Black Swan* (2010) did not arrive for another two years. It's reasonable to assume that if *The Wrestler* tanked at the box office, its follow-up wouldn't have been made. Although Aronofsky originally envisioned one single movie about a wrestler and a ballerina, during development he came to the realization that these were two distinctly different worlds, and Aronofsky decided to split the story into two movies.[xxxviii] The respective films credit different writers, but *The Wrestler* and *Black Swan* are impeccably aligned: two entertainers, both relying on their bodies to perform, experiencing self-doubt. *The Wrestler* showcases an aging man at the end of a lustrous career; *Black Swan* showcases a young woman preparing for the break-out performance of her career.

Some articles around the time of *Revolutionary Road*'s debut (December 2008) mention that Mendes was in the process of editing *Away We Go*. When *Away We Go* made it to theaters six months later (June 2009), Mendes declared that it was, in fact, a companion piece to *Revolutionary Road*. Mendes explains in numerous interviews that directing the two films back-to-back allowed him to craft *Revolutionary Road* and *Away We Go* into complimentary movies.

EARLY 1950s VS. LATE 2000s

Some literary scholars consider the novel, *Revolutionary Road* by Richard Yates, a classic. It even landed a place on TIME magazine's top 100 greatest novels of all time.[xxxix] However, Mendes intended for *Revolutionary Road* to translate to a modern audience. Despite his versatility in genre, Mendes' appears to be in familiar territory as the resemblances between *American Beauty* and *Revolutionary Road* are striking: suburban settings, productions viewed as "Oscar-bait," and the theme of real estate via Annette Bening and Kathy Bates' characters. However, the most prominent shared feature are the stories of two men trapped in the corporate world, wanting to escape their cubicles. There is juxtaposition in their outcomes: Kevin Spacey improves his self-image and finds paternal solace; DiCaprio on the other hand, remains closed-minded and broken.

Away We Go also showcases the suburbs, but what sets it apart from Mendes' other family-driven films is that the couple, played by John Krasinski and Maya Rudolph, function as witnesses. The traveling pair observe a variety of families (including their own, respectively) trying to decide on a new home to raise a baby. It's worth highlighting director Hal Ashby's influence on Mendes, in how some places, settings, and locations become more fascinating than the characters. Ashby's *The Last Detail* (1973), a movie centering on three sailors finding themselves in bizarre locations with odd people over an extended weekend, was the primary inspiration for Mendes. The three Navymen experience awkward, albeit humorous encounters with a variety of people throughout the course of *The Last Detail*, similar to the main couple in *Away We Go*.

Similarly, Krasinski and Rudolph are so focused on becoming parents, they move past what's going on around them without really taking notice. In interviews and audio-commentary, Mendes repeatedly states that "Krasinski and Rudolph don't move - rather, the world moves around them." The leading couple does not concern themselves with the world in which they exist. When on a college campus, they pass by a student protest where a banner in the background reads: "The CIA trained bin Laden", yet the couple walks past it without batting an eye.[xl]

With the exception of the protest banner (if you notice it), *Away We Go* refuses to participate in its era: there is no social media, no pop-culture references, no smartphones, no politics, and no terrorism. The locations of *Away We Go* are authentic places that a contemporary American audience can identify with, contrary to *Revolutionary Road,* which displays the 1950s for the audience, making the nostalgic era part of the story. For example, DiCaprio's time spent in Paris during the war is reminiscent of the post-WWII era. The film showcases the technology of the 1950s: the casual smoking, the work attire, and the constant drinking. Mendes highlights that "on one level, [*Revolutionary Road* is] an exploration of the '50s, an exploration of that period - but it's not about the '50s. To me it's a very contemporary story, it's a very modern story that deals with very, very modern concerns. The story is about the relationship, and this story is as true now as it was 40 years ago, without a question."[xli]

MASCULINITY IN CRISIS AND STAR PERSONA

Perhaps the biggest juxtaposition of the two films are the characters portrayed by Leonardo DiCaprio and John Krasinski. Side-by-side they make a poignant and ironic commentary about American masculinity. The appearance of Leonardo DiCaprio's dashing, polished exterior contrasts John Krasinski's disheveled, quirky attire. Their morals differ: DiCaprio lies and talks down to his wife, whereas Krasinski exudes unconditional love for his girlfriend. Even their character arcs are inverse reflections of each other; DiCaprio's final onscreen moment displays a broken father, while Krasinski emanates paternal fortitude.

The 50s DiCaprio (Frank Wheeler) is a more intrinsically dressed young businessman, well-postured, and able to make conversation with seemingly anyone he meets regardless of age or gender. A subtle yet poignant moment is DiCaprio's conversation with a mentally unstable former mathematician, played by Michael Shannon, upon his first visit to Shannon's home. When tensions seem to be rising, DiCaprio handles the socially awkward Shannon maturely, treating him with respect.

The quirky John Krasinski (Burt), on the other hand, doesn't own a coordinated wardrobe. Nothing of Krasinski's appearance would convince a random bystander that he's material for the ideal professional. Additionally, whenever Krasinski gets a job-related call, he changes his tone of voice to sound "big business," an idiosyncratic behavior that anyone watching can see is only for show. One could even argue that Krasinski performing cunnilingus on Maya Rudolph in the opening scene is evidence that he is the subordinate of the couple. There is an endearing quality of Burt/Krasinski that leads the audience (as well as the other characters) to warm up to him. He's so oblivious to his own eccentricities that once you get past the visual appearance, a decent, loving man appears.

Casting is a crucial element in the filmmaking process and in this case, a clear indicator of the duality of the two movies. Leonardo DiCaprio had proven his remarkable acting ability in the early 1990s, and throughout the mid-2000s graduated from boyish typecast into a virile, A-list superstar. *Revolutionary Road* didn't have to work hard to strike up media buzz; the anticipated reunion of the iconic *Titanic* screen couple was enough to adorn magazine covers. Additionally, prior to *Revolutionary Road*'s limited and wide releases, Leonardo DiCaprio had already been nominated for Best Actor by the Golden Globes.[14] However, the general public was most likely unaware that Frank Wheeler, DiCaprio's character, was an emotionally weak and chauvinistic man--a character who would make a modern audience (and/or reader) cringe at his behavior towards his wife. Usually, the general movie-going audience does not like to see their favorite celebrities play deplorable human beings, so DiCaprio's casting was ideal for inciting an intentional but bitter reaction towards the character.

Revolutionary Road showcases the couple's frustration of being surrounded by a dull, suburban lifestyle. In an attempt to escape mundane suburbia, Kate Winslet (April Wheeler) works out a considerable solution that

---

[14] The Golden Globe nominees were announced Thursday, December 11th, 2008.
Revolutionary Road released on Friday, December 26th at only a handful of theaters. It was expanded to formal wide release on Friday, January 23rd, 2009.

suits both her and her husband: albeit bold, she suggests moving from their banal Connecticut suburb overseas to Paris. Leonardo DiCaprio, before knowing his wife's plan, handles his frustration by indulging in an affair with a girl from his office. From the beginning, the couple are in poor contrast: Winslet's proposed solution is mindful of her husband, whereas DiCaprio's affair reflects self-gratification. When their plan to move to Paris begins to fall apart, due to DiCaprio's pay raise and Winslet's pregnancy, DiCaprio makes the logical argument that to remain in the United States is more financially secure. For the well-being of the family's living situation, DiCaprio's argument is, indeed, valid.

Yet DiCaprio/Frank's moral compass is askew; while righteously opposing the idea of abortion, he continually speaks down to his wife, doubts her decisions, and believes his opinion is always superior. When confessing the affair to April/Winslet, she is already emotionally broken:

APRIL

```
Would it be alright if we didn't talk about anything?
Can't we just take each day as it comes, and do the best
we can, and not feel we have to talk about everything
all the time?
```

He smiles patiently.

FRANK

```
I don't think I suggested we talk about everything all
the time. My point was, we've both been under a strain
and we ought to be trying to help each other as much as
we can right now.
```

She's utterly uninterested and it's making him nervous.

FRANK (CONT'D)

```
I mean God knows my own behavior has been pretty weird
lately... I mean, as it happens... there is actually
something I'd like to tell you about...
```

She continues folding the napkins.

FRANK (CONT'D)

```
I've been with a girl in the city a few times.
```

Finally, she stops moving. She looks at him.

FRANK (CONT'D)

A girl I hardly even know. It was nothing to me, but she got a little carried away. She's just a kid... Anyway, it's over now. It's really over. If I weren't sure of that I guess I could never have told you about it.

APRIL

Why did you?

FRANK
(relieved)
Baby, I don't know. I think it was a simple case of wanting to be a man again after all that abortion business. Some kind of neurotic, irrational need to prove something.

APRIL

No. I don't mean why did you have the girl; I mean why did you tell me about it?

He is suddenly unsure.

APRIL

I mean what's the point? Is it supposed to make me jealous, or something? Is it supposed to make me fall in love with you, or back into bed with you, or what? I mean what am I supposed to say?

He tries that same patient smile, but it's not convincing.

FRANK

Why don't you say what you feel?

APRIL

I don't feel anything.

FRANK

In other words you don't care what I do or who I fuck or anything?

APRIL

No; I guess that's right; I don't.

She is frighteningly calm.

APRIL (CONT'D)

Fuck who you like.

The tension mounts, but the fight is put on hold, as the mentally unstable Michael Shannon arrives with his parents for dinner at the Wheeler's house. If there are two single scenes that link *Revolutionary Road* with *Away We Go*, the fights over dinner are the clearest showcase of DiCaprio's and Krasinski's masculinity on trial.

DINNER OUTBURSTS

Returning to Darren Aronofsky's *The Wrestler* and *Black Swan*, scenes between the two films are constructed as parallels. For example, *The Wrestler* ends with a cheering crowd, then hard cut to black; *Black Swan* ends with an applauding audience, and a slow fade to white. The two dinner scenes in *Revolutionary Road* and *Away We Go* portray the contrast between both couples so well, that it's worth watching the scenes back-to-back. Both scenes are almost exactly 4 minutes and 30 seconds long.

"I'M GLAD I'M NOT GONNA BE THAT KID"

Literary scholars praise Richard Yates' novel for the character of John Givings, played by Michael Shannon. The insane man speaks without censoring himself and is able to see past the flaws of suburban life. This tense setting in which Michael Shannon arrives (just after DiCaprio/Frank admits his affair) is ripe for him to prod the couple on why they have decided against leaving the suburbs. Shannon, who can read people brilliantly, realizes that Winslet/April feels a mixture of sadness and anger about their current living situation, so he turns his hostile behavior towards DiCaprio/Frank, probing to reveal the underlying tension.

Shannon becomes combative towards DiCaprio, and his hostile words sting because there is truth in what he says. The more outlandish insults ("I bet he knocked her up on purpose just so he can spend the rest of his life hiding behind a maternity dress, that way he'd ever have to find out what he's really made of.") are what ultimately push DiCaprio over the edge. Slamming his fist on the table and rising, DiCaprio outburst only embarrasses himself. DiCaprio/Frank's backlash is not just targeted at Shannon, but also at his mother (Kathy Bates), who tries to rationalize that Shannon is mentally not well. DiCaprio lacks the maturity to ignore the insults and lets Shannon's poisonous words internally wreck him.

Getting up to leave, Shannon mockingly says to Winslet: "Big family man you have there. I feel sorry for you. Still, maybe you deserve each other, I mean, the way you look right now, I'm beginning to feel for him too. You must give him a pretty bad time if making babies is the only way he can prove he's got a pair of balls." Shannon's insulting remarks are spoken to Winslet, knowing that DiCaprio can hear him. By insulting her gloomy appearance, Shannon indirectly attacks DiCaprio's masculinity. Again, a reasonable person would ignore these low-blows, knowing they are spoken just out of spite, but the fact that DiCaprio yells again and threatens to hit him is pathetic--a rational man would never act that way over petty remarks. Trying to leave the house, Shannon makes a mock apology followed by a bold prophecy, saying that he's "Glad I'm not going to be that kid," pointing towards Winslet and the child who will be aborted the next day.

The incident causes the couple's deterioration. DiCaprio cannot let it go -- he defaults to talking too much, defending himself, and remaining chauvinistic towards her: "Well you're wrong, April." DiCaprio doesn't utilize Shannon's malicious, yet accurate observation for self-examination; rather, it becomes a launch-pad for their biggest fight yet, one that convinces Winslet to attempt an abortion.

"HEY WOLFIE, WANNA GET IN THE STROLLER?"

A similar scenario is presented in *Away We Go*, although handled differently, by a mature, strong couple. Both what Michael Shannon and Maggie Gyllenhaal say in their respected scenes is uncomfortable, but keeping in mind that *Away We Go* is a comedy, it's "okay" for the audience to laugh at the inappropriateness of the stroller scene. The mise-en-scene itself is comical, placing the modest Krasinski and Rudolph in the setting of an upper-middle class dining room, surrounded by candles and fancy wine glasses.

There is a significant juxtaposition in the type of discomfort felt when watching Michael Shannon insult Leonardo DiCaprio's sexuality vs. watching Maggie Gyllenhaal allude to the pain of giving birth as being "so enlightening," adding "and now, having experienced childbirth, I watch CNN and I feel like I understand war." Krasinski calmly and respectfully asks to cease conversing about babies and parenthood, and the subject changes to Krasinski's work. Previously in *Away We Go*, Krasinski/Burt admits to enjoying what he does for a living, despite it being a mundane job. Roderick/Josh Hamilton becomes downright condescending -- arguably worse than Michael Shannon in that he's not clinically insane. Here we see another parallel to *Revolutionary Road,* when Hamilton (like Shannon) doesn't speak to Krasinski directly, instead he talks to his toddler, Wolfie, knowing that Krasinski will hear him.

Despite Krasinski's living coming under attack by the new age couple, it isn't until Maggie Gyllenhaal talks down to Maya Rudolph/Verona that Krasinski is sent over the edge and literally takes a stand (as does DiCaprio). *Away We Go* showcases a healthy relationship; Krasinski's more aggressive behavior is complemented by Rudolph, who joins to leave. DiCaprio's outburst defends himself; Krasinski's outburst defends his woman. Furthermore, Krasinski's outburst is not a rant or slew of insults thrown back--instead, he wisely evades: "If I have to explain it to you looney tunes, just forget it."

Another significant difference is that Krasinski ends the confrontation perfectly; he gets in that one last "thing", the last "oomph", the final touch that DiCaprio can never achieve. Krasinski walks back into the house with a stroller (the gift that previously offended the new-age couple) and offers their toddler, Wolfie, a ride. The viewer cheers Krasinski's behavior, as opposed to the way the audience dreads anytime DiCaprio starts speaking. The most poignant moment is a short reaction shot of Maya Rudolph laughing at what Krasinski is doing. Rudolph clearly loves this response, as he jogs out the door with the stroller. Imagine DiCaprio in the same situation and responding the same way: Winslet would never approve of that behavior, as their disdainful attitudes towards each other prevent a shared sense of humor.

FINAL SCENES

Leonardo DiCaprio, Hollywood's most popular actor, exits *Revolutionary Road* without pride. His final moment shows him on a park bench while his children play on the swings. For the first time in *Revolutionary Road*, DiCaprio has a scene alone with his children. The short moment is incredibly opaque, leaving room for interpretation: have his priorities been refocused? Has DiCaprio put himself through an examination of conscience? Has he learned any lessons? Will he re-marry? The melancholy ending of *Revolutionary Road* is drastically contrasted to the triumphant ending of *Away We Go*.

Once again, considering the casting of actor John Krasinski in 2009, who was not a dominating cinematic presence like Leonardo DiCaprio. Yet his character, Burt, in *Away We Go* is a far more inspirational character than DiCaprio's Frank Wheeler; the audience is given a genuine, honest, and enjoyable human being who legitimately cares about his girlfriend and others.

The final powerful minutes of *Away We Go* show Krasinski and Rudolph arriving at the house which they plan on moving into. What complements the scene, and the whole film, is Krasinski walking to the other end of the house and opening the backdoor, physically and metaphorically breaking open their future. His actions may seem routine, yet they are metaphorically very masculine--the soon-to-be father prepping the house. Sitting on the back porch, Krasinski announces the house is "perfect" for them. Krasinski tenderly takes her hand and kisses it, an action that showcases their strength and his role of caretaker and provider. Krasinski and Rudolph exit *Away We Go* together with tears of joy, a child on the way, and a prosperous future.

Sam Mendes responds to the domestic instability of *American Beauty* and *Revolutionary Road* with an antidote in *Away We Go*. Self-examination, devotion, support, and selflessness are keys to prosperity in modern society. The vicious circle of suburbia drama can be defeated.

SKYFALL AND SPECTRE (FINAL 10 MINUTES)

THE REAL ORIGIN STORY

Comic book author Stan Lee published a narrative in 1962 about a scientist exposed to gamma radiation, that resulted in the scientist transforming into a green monster, known as the Incredible Hulk. The following year, Lee co-authored another character: a billionaire arms dealer who realizes that his weapons are being misused by foreign governments. The wealthy playboy takes matters into his own hands by becoming the vigilante, Iron Man. The rejuvenation of comic-book films have made these two "Avengers" well known in modern pop culture, yet the origin stories are not the reasons **how** or **why** the Hulk and Iron Man came into existence. The usage of radiation, weapons of mass destruction, and corporate crime was Stan Lee's ways of contemplating Cold War fears of the 1960s. A scientist turning into a green monster may make for good fiction, but it doesn't quite resonate with the modern audience in the same way. Iron Man specifically underwent an adaptation that incorporated terrorism from the Middle East and engage the audience's obsession with technology. Dr. Laurence Knapp points out that "[Jon Favreau's 2008] Iron Man is perfectly suited for the late-2000s in that he's a superhero simply because he controls his technology so well. How often does the modern person have trouble working their iPads? Iron Man practically has an iPad strapped to his chest."

The character of James Bond likewise, was created for a specific time period, but also sustained a strong, consistent following. James Bond first appeared in April 1953, in the book *Casino Royale* by Ian Fleming, which sold over 10,000 copies in its first year of publication. Fleming wrote another 11 novels and various short stories about James Bond until his death in 1964. The first feature-length motion picture, *Dr. No* (1962, Terence Young) achieved success that would consistently increase in box-office gross with each new film.[15] With each new 007 film, the cast, themes, and styles were adapted to cater to an audience with ever-changing agendas. The four Daniel Craig films, *Casino Royale*; *Quantum of Solace*; *Skyfall*; and *Spectre* were produced with the intention of keeping the stories as character-driven as Fleming's novels, yet situated within the post-9/11 world, as opposed to Fleming's vantage point of post-WWII Great Britain.

FALL OF THE BRITISH EMPIRE

In July, 1939, Ian Fleming became involved with Great Britain's Royal Navy, primarily in the field of code breaking. He would eventually work with the United States' covert intelligence service throughout the war until the summer of 1945. Afterwards, Fleming wrote for *The Sunday Times*, a newspaper in the town of Kemsley, about 50 miles east of London. Eight years would pass between the end of World War II to when Fleming would publish *Casino Royale*. Despite Great Britain being on the winning side of World War II, the country suffered a devastating loss. The death toll in Great Britain was approximately 450,900 (383,700 military and 67,200 civilian) not counting the deaths in

---

[15] *Dr. No* (1962, Terence Young) earned $16.0 million; *From Russia with Love* (1963, Terence Young) $24.7 million; *Goldfinger* (1964, Guy Hamilton), $51.0 million; and *Thunderball* (1965, Terence Young), $63.5 million. Adjusting the box-office numbers for inflation, *Thunderball* and *Goldfinger* still remain the highest grossing 007 films.

countries under its governance at the time[16]. The economy was badly dependent on loans from the United States, which had come to Great Britain's economic and military aid during the war. Additionally, British morale was low for failing to keep the Nazis in check prior to Adolf Hitler's invasion across Europe. The destruction to London, especially the city's ports laid devastation to one of the world's great cities. With the United States receiving credit for turning the tide of battle, winning the war, and coming out as the dominant world power, the perception of what was once the prestigious British empire was disappearing. James Bond was Fleming's way of addressing this.

Fleming's irritation with Britain's beaten pride is subliminally present in the majority of the 007 novels. For example, the quipping between James Bond and his boss, M, who is elder, highlights the generational gaps between the World War I era and the World War II era. One of the book's recurring characters is an American agent whose help is often invaluable to Bond, emphasizing how Great Britain had become dependent on U.S. assistance.[17] Ron Falzone, associate professor of Cinema Arts + Sciences at Columbia College Chicago, points to the film *You Only Live Twice* (1967, Lewis Gilbert) as an indicator of Great Britain's lowered stature: "Bond is sent in as a negotiator between the Japanese and the hijackers. It shows how Great Britain's role on the world stage has been reduced; they can no longer handle the crisis themselves. Furthermore, Bond spends a lot time in the film adapting and learning the ways of the East."

The movie franchise explored different themes in the subsequent decades. As skillfully explained in the popular media blog *The Nerdist*: "While keeping the general themes, the Bond films delved into different film genres including slapstick humor [*Diamond Are Forever*], self-parody, blaxploitation [*Live and Let Die*], kung fu movie [*The Man with the Golden Gun*], and even, by the decade's end, space adventure science fiction [*Moonraker*]. It was a period of experimentation for the series and the audience lapped it up."[xlii] With regards

---

[16] Burma, India, Malta, and Newfoundland

[17] The character of Felix Leiter periodically appeared in both the books and films.

to the 1980s: "All five films in the '80s[18] are straight-up big stunt action movies and they never get too silly or stray too far from the main throughline."[xliii]

"A CHARACTER RIPPED FROM THE HEADLINES"

It's important to keep in mind that Sam Mendes inherited a brand, the 007 dynasty. Hired to direct the third Daniel Craig film, Mendes is given a specific "James Bond" that has already been customized for the contemporary culture. The "James Bond" that Daniel Craig portrays complements his fellow contemporaries: Christian Bale as Batman, and Matt Damon as Jason Bourne. The trio of James Bond, Jason Bourne, and Batman became the new standard for characters in the post-9/11 cinema throughout the 2000s. Moreover, Sam Mendes finds himself in company with fellow British directors Christopher Nolan and Paul Greengrass in handling a character from decades past and restructuring him for a contemporary audience.

As James Bond has been periodically reevaluated since his 1960's debut, so too has Batman, whose television show (1966-1968, totaling 120 episodes) seems rather absurd by today's standards. The series was released during the American pop art phase, sharing airtime with shows like *Bewitched* (1964-1972) and *The Beverly Hillbillies* (1962-1971), so the show's eccentricities were appropriate for the time. The late 60s Batman was short-lived, as the cynical 1970s was not going to accept a rich, WASP-y man (and his young protégé) fighting crime. The character didn't resurface until the late 80s when Warner Bros. attempted a motion picture adaptation that departed from the 60's style in favor of a darker approach. Dr. Knapp accurately points out, "The 80s dictated

---

[18] *For Your Eyes Only* (1981, John Glen); *Octopussy* (1983, John Glen); *Never Say Never Again* (1983, Irvin Kershner); *A View to Kill* (1985, John Glen); *The Living Daylights* (1987, John Glen); and *License to Kill* (1989, John Glen).

that Batman cannot prance around in gray spandex tights. He had to be upgraded to black metal gear."

Despite box-office success throughout the 1990s, the Batman films received increasingly poor reviews, leading adult audiences to become disenchanted with Hollywood's Batman.[19] James Bond would share a similar fate, as the 007 films of the late 1990s were also greeted with a lukewarm response. Fan's and audience's displeasure with *The World Is Not Enough* (1999, Michael Apted) and *Die Another Day* (2002, Lee Tamahori) left the franchise at an awkward stance due to the increasing jadedness of the late 1990s, followed by the trauma of terrorism in the post-9/11 world.

The 1990s frivolous James Bond and Batman films, existing in a social climate concern with the global threat of terrorism made poor contrast. The eccentricities slumped in comparison to the sharper *The Bourne Identity* (2002, Doug Liman) which became one of two hugely influential films of the decade. Based off a 1980's novel, the story was adapted for a modern audience and touched on issues of government secrecy. The positive reception to *The Bourne Identity* allowed for a sequel, in which the producers hired new director, Paul Greengrass who redefine the genre further. With a background in documentary filmmaking, Greengrass shot *The Bourne Supremacy* (2004) with handheld cameras and cut the film with a hyper-edited aesthetic, giving the sequel its own unique, visceral style. Greengrass intentionally used close-ups on Matt Damon, emphasizing the story's focus on him,[xliv] creating a character-driven plot. By placing Matt Damon's/Bourne's emotions at the forefront, government conspiracy and politics linger as the backdrop of the film. This orchestration encourages the viewer to sympathize with Matt Damon's/Bourne's pain, frustration, and rage, helping make the fictional setting feel like the modern world. This helped give the Bourne franchise a sense of, what Greengrass

---

[19] Tim Burton's *Batman* earned $251.1 million in the domestic box office, becoming the highest grossing film of 1989. The sequels consecutively, *Batman Returns* (1992, Tim Burton) earning $162.8 million; *Batman Forever* (1995, Joel Schumacher) earning $184 million; *Batman & Robin* (1997, Joel Schumacher) earning $107.3 million. Despite the progressively negative reviews, the prosperity of *Batman: The Animated Series* (1992-1995) lead to multiple spin-offs including animated movies, merchandise, and video games. The series continued in *Batman Beyond* (1999-2001), keeping the character(s) culturally relevant as the 2000s began.

famously called, "a character ripped from the headlines." The Batman and James Bond franchises quickly followed suit.

Batman experienced a resurgence in the wake of the comic book revival of the 2000s with *Batman Begins* (2005, Christopher Nolan), which reframed the story in a more realistic context, avoiding science fiction-based explanations. The execution of an intellectually sophisticated, darker narrative was what the comic book genre needed to balance against the superfluous *Spider-Man* imitation flicks. *The Bourne Supremacy* and *Batman Begins* were indicators that to attract mass audiences, the films not only had to be darker, but more emotionally driven and plausible within the current social climate. The increased monetary and critical success of the sequels, *The Bourne Ultimatum* (2007, Paul Greengrass) and *The Dark Knight* (2008, Christopher Nolan) are evidence of what the standard for blockbuster films were in the late 2000s.[xlv]

For 2006's *Casino Royale*, the intention was to reboot the story of James Bond appropriately using Ian Fleming's first novel. The goal was to integrate the emotion from Fleming's book into the story, straying away from the campiness established in previous Bond films. Casting Daniel Craig (who doesn't look like any of the actors who previously played the part) gave a fresh face to a franchise in the process of deconstructing itself. Craig's acting background ensured that James Bond's emotions would be the central focus. As Craig himself points out: "I'm not lying when I say that the only way to do that is to forget it's a 'Bond' movie. Get on and make the best movie you can - all the 'Bond' sort of sorts itself out."[xlvi]

Casino Royale removed the nonsensical behavior of the 1990s, and replaced it with Daniel Craig withstanding both physical and emotional pain. The sequel, *Quantum of Solace* (2008, Marc Foster) showcased Craig's pain turning into revenge. *Quantum of Solace* borrowed from the Jason Bourne movies by incorporating current social issues, like the contemporary hot-button concern of environmental protection; the filmmakers also used handheld cameras, resulting in a similar aesthetic to *The Bourne Supremacy* and *The Bourne Ultimatum*.

RESURRECTION

As Mendes' directorial career in film has been built upon character-driven plots, he was the perfect hire for *Skyfall* and *Spectre*, as both films remained truer to the character-driven plots of Ian Fleming's novels. Following the trends of the time, Mendes would reference *The Dark Knight* as inspiration for *Skyfall*:

> "What Christopher Nolan proved was that you can make a huge movie that is thrilling and entertaining and has a lot to say about the world we live in, even if, in the case with The Dark Knight, it's not even set in our world. It felt like a movie that was about our world post-9/11 and played on our fears and discussed our fears and why they existed... That did help give me the confidence to take this movie [Skyfall]in directions that, without The Dark Knight, might not have been possible."xlvii

The character of James Bond goes through a death & resurrection in the two final novels: Bond is abandoned with amnesia at the end of *You Only Live Twice* and returns, brainwashed, at the beginning of *The Man with the Golden Gun*. For *Skyfall*, Daniel Craig's assumed death is short lived, and the story fixates on his aging (to attempt amnesia would seem forgery of the popular Jason Bourne films). The concept of **resurrection** is accented with a doppelganger: Javier Bardem. *Skyfall* presents a version of what Daniel Craig <u>could</u> <u>have</u> returned as. Bardem first appears wearing white, contrasting Craig's usual dark colors; Bardem is openly dismissive of MI6, gadgets, chases, thrills -- elements that are themselves paradigms of the 007 franchise.

Bond/Craig's definitive resurrection comes at the end of Act II/beginning of Act III in *Skyfall*. Throughout *Casino Royale* and *Quantum of Solace* (and the majority of *Skyfall*) we see a disgruntled agent who reluctantly takes orders. Craig's James Bond will occasionally do whatever he wants, however he's always in the position of hunting something or someone. *Casino Royale,* for instance, features two thrilling chases which lead to a high-stakes poker game in an attempt to bring an illegal arms dealer to justice. By *Quantum of Solace,* although Craig is driven by revenge, he's still trailing behind the same secret organization. The major shift between the character seen in the prequels and the "resurrected James Bond," who hijacks the rest of the *Skyfall* even bleeding into *Spectre,* happens during Judi Dench's court-mandated hearing about the reliability and necessity of the MI6 secret-agent program. Moments before Javier Bardem ambushes the hearing, Dench recites a poem by Alfred Lord Tennyson in her closing statements:

> "We are not now that strength, which in old days moved earth and heaven. That which we are we are. One equal temper of heroic hearts, made weak by and time and fate, but strong in will. To strive, to seek, to find, and not to yield."

Although Dench's words are meant to address the MI6 program, they are used as a voice over to the image of Daniel Craig running out of the subway; a Christ-like resurrection rising from the ground. Not only does Daniel Craig commandeer Judi Dench, but the film's story as well, taking Dench to the rural house where he was raised. The vast majority of the 007 films conclude with a finale of James Bond having to infiltrate the villain's lair. *Skyfall* is the reverse in that Daniel Craig wants to battle Javier Bardem on his own turf.

After Craig and Dench arrive at the Skyfall estate, the house curator, played by Albert Finney, points to another resurrection motif. Finney shows Dench a small alcove to run to in danger, and he notes that the cave is where, as a child, Craig retreated to in mourning. Finney explains: "The night I told him his parents had died, he hid in here for two days. When he did come out, he wasn't a boy anymore." The camera holds on a silent Judi Dench, as she stares intently at the birthplace of her most ferocious agent.

Skyfall's clever way of paying homage to the 007 franchise, while building strong story structure is an element that Professor Falzone credits Mendes' directing for:

> "The Bond series has a history of employing directors who were technicians by trait. These were not directors who were schooled in storytelling, which is why the films got more violent

and spectacular in their stunts. However, Sam Mendes coming from a theatre background, where a huge emphasis is placed on the text, he's able to translate the story to screen so effectively that the audience finds themselves moved by the drama, especially the death of M [Judi Dench]. Bond movies are not supposed to make people cry, however Skyfall can pull that off."

THE POST-SNOWDEN ERA

As the culture distanced itself from 9/11 and the Iraq War, as well as gained some amount of closure with the death of Usama bin Laden, resentment to the Patriot Act,[20] began to arise. In the summer of 2013, CIA analyst Edward Snowden leaked evidence proving the National Security Agency was using **mass surveillance** programs that violated information privacy laws. Concerns about the Patriot Act were brought to the forefront by a "real spy," earning Snowden a wide range of names from "patriot" to "traitor". Cinema's two most popular spies utilized the cultural reaction to Edward Snowden as inspiration for *Spectre* and *Jason Bourne* (2016, Paul Greengrass).

Technology is a crucial element of the 007 gadget-obsessed films, and Mendes resists the novelty of gizmos, stating that the modern audience has gadget(s) in form or another on their smart phones.[xlviii] Technology is creatively "re-cast" as the villain. For the first half of *Skyfall*, Bardem is present in the form of a taunting computer virus. He's able to communicate with Judi Dench, telling her to "think on your sins," while also causing mayhem by blowing up the MI6 building and revealing the identity of undercover agents. The power of mass-

---

[20] Formal title: "Uniting and Strengthening America by Providing Appropriate Tools Required to Intercept and Obstruct Terrorism Act of 2001." A month following the 9/11 attacks, congress and President George W. Bush passed the Patriot Act into law, which gave the FBI and CIA a significant amount of leniency to spy on whoever they deemed necessary.

surveillance is the initial threat in *Spectre* in its ability to infiltrate the political realm and ability to use fear to manipulate governments. As the obsession over the control of nuclear weapons was the purpose for the original S.P.E.C.T.R.E. (short for "Special Executive for Counterintelligence, Terrorism, Revenge and Extortion") in the 1960's novels and movies, the ability to access everyone's computer becomes the leading fear tactic in the 2010s.

Released less than a year apart, *Spectre* and *Jason Bourne* complement each other well; in both films, technology is used as a weapon to infringe upon people's privacy. *Jason Bourne* addresses the concept from the standpoint of social media, showing a government demanding a backdoor entrance to gather data from the common man. Both Matt Damon's and Daniel Craig's characters discover their lives have been manipulated by larger organizations since their first movies. Although Damon is manipulated for the benefit of the U.S. government, Craig is spied on as the target of revenge. The concept of the past catching up with Craig is the theme of *Spectre*'s title song, "Writing's on the Wall":

> "I've been here before but always hit the floor. I've spent a lifetime running, and I always get away... I feel like a storm is coming. If I'm gonna make it through the day, then there's not more use in running, this is something I gotta face."

Similar to Matt Damon's discoveries in *Jason Bourne*, Craig's discovery that his life has been tracked reveals a villainous mastermind. Christoph Waltz, cast as the quintessential Bond-villain, Ernst Stavro Blofeld, builds a personal accord with Craig. Waltz uses mass-surveillance to argue he is the alpha-male between the two of them by being able to hack into MI6 closed circuit television:

BLOFELD

Well, James, it looks like you're all alone.

BOND

Not much more than a voyeur, are you? Too scared to join in.

BLOFELD

I don't think you quite understand.

                              BOND

Oh, I think I do. You set cities on fire and watch
innocent people burn, so you can convince governments to
join an intelligence network you've paid for. Not that
complicated. I'm guessing our little friend, C, he's one
of your disciples.

                            BLOFELD

You could say that.

                              BOND

And what does he get out of it?

                            BLOFELD

Nothing. He's a visionary, like me.

                              BOND

Visionaries. Psychiatric wards are full of them.

                            BLOFELD

Whereas you couldn't see what's right in front of you.
You came across me so many times and yet you never saw
me. Le Chiffre, Greene, Silva.

                              BOND

All dead.

                            BLOFELD

Yeah, that's right. A nice pattern developed. You
interfered in my world, I destroyed yours. Or did you
think it was coincidence that all the women in your life
ended up dead? Vesper Lynd, for example.

Blofeld pauses, turns to Madeleine

                      BLOFELD (CONT'D)

She was the big one. Has he told you about her?

Returning to Bond

                      BLOFELD (CONT'D)

And then, of course, your beloved M. Gone forever. Me.
It was all me, James. It's always been me. The author
of all your pain.

Blofeld warmly looks to Madeleine

                        BLOFELD (cont'd)
     You're a brave woman, my dear.

He taps a button on his tablet. The lights in the room dim. Those
sitting at computer terminals surrounding the room stop and stand in
attention.

                        MADELEINE
     Now I understand why my father lost his mind.

                        BLOFELD
     He didn't lose his mind, he was just weak. But at least
     he understood what he was up against. You see, they
     failed to comprehend the crucial fact, that a terrible
     event can lead to something wonderful. Since you mention
     your father, I'll show you.

Blofeld taps another button on his tablet.

Monitors around the hall begin playing a black and white video
recording, taken from a hidden camera.

                        MR. WHITE (O.S.)
     She's clever. She's smarter than me. She knows how to
     hide.

The conversation between Bond and Mr. White as taken from the security
camera plays.

                        BOND (O.S.)
     I can protect her if you tell me where he is. I can keep
     her alive.

                        MR. WHITE (O.S.)
     Yeah.

                        BOND (O.S.)
     You have my word.

Madeline walks closer to one of the monitors.

Bond immediately concerned, knowing exactly what Blofeld intends to
show Madeline - instantly aware of the damage the video will cause
Madeline.

                              BOND
No, no, no. Turn this off.

                         MR. WHITE (O.S.)
Your word? The word of an assassin!

                              BOND
                            (Angrier)
Turn this off.

                            BLOFELD
This is important.

Bond turns and rushes Blofeld.

                              BOND
                            (yelling)
I said turn it off!

A bodyguard extends a baton and quickly hits Bond's knee, knocking
him face-down on the floor.

                            BLOFELD
I want you to understand something.

                           BOND (O.S.)
That's my word.

Bond, pained, slowly looks up. He turns his attention to Madeleine
who's absorbed by the video.

                              BOND
Madeleine? Look at me. Don't look at him, Madeleine.
Look at me.

Madeleine with tears in her eyes turns from the monitors and looks at
Bond. The video continues to play in the background.

                         MR. WHITE (O.S.)
L'Américain. You save her, she can lead you to
L'Américain. She knows L'Américain. Try the Hoffler
Klinik. You're a kite dancing in a hurricane, Mr. Bond.
So long.

The gunshot from the video is heard. Bond's and Madeline's eyes remain
locked on one another.

In keeping the films close to Fleming's original novels, the relationships Daniel Craig has with the women in *Skyfall* and *Spectre* challenge the sexualized "Bond-Girl" stereotype of a half-hearted sidekick. In the majority of the novels, Bond is able to understand and delicately "unlock" a woman. Bérénice Marlohe in *Skyfall* appears as the typical femme-fatale, but once Craig is in close proximity with her, he smoothly picks her apart and unveils that she's actually terrified of the mysterious Javier Bardem. The same tactic is repeated in *Spectre* with both Monica Bellucci and Léa Seydoux, as Craig first seeks them out, and then convinces the ladies to disclose details about the Spectre organization. Of all the "Bond Girls" in the Daniel Craig films, Seydoux remains paramount because she is not just a pawn; as Christoph Waltz points out, Seydoux is "the daughter of an assassin, the only one who could have understood him."

Spectre appropriately partners Daniel Craig and Léa Seydoux as a definitive couple, as Seydoux doesn't allow the dark organization to trap her, as the previous women in the series; Craig also does not kill for her sake. After pinning Waltz at gunpoint, Craig is taunted by the villainous mastermind to "finish it" and shoot him dead. Craig can follow Waltz's direction, but it would continue the cycle of violence which the Spectre organization endorses. Instead, Craig unloads his gun ("out of bullets") and walks away, letting Ralph Fiennes take over with Waltz's arrest. The finale harkens back to the theme of the Patriot Act as Fiennes tells Waltz, "Under the special measures act of 2001, I'm detaining you on behalf of her majesty's government."

SAM MENDES' AUTHORSHIP

With respect to Sam Mendes' authorship, *Spectre* is the first time that he intentionally repeats himself. "Until I did these two, [*Skyfall* and *Spectre*] every movie I directed was the absolute polar opposite of the one before it. That was not random; it is a deliberate attempt to not repeat myself, and to challenge myself with different stylistic challenges. That is how it is done with filmmakers I most admire."

The intention of creating a diverse resume, including directing two blockbuster sequels, bridges back to the "bank loaned" Academy Award. While promoting *Spectre*, Sam Mendes made it explicitly clear that his shifting filmography has always been intentional since *American Beauty*:

> "I thought, I'm going to earn this Oscar, but it is going to happen over 20, 30 years of filmmaking. No sane person could process it otherwise... can you imagine me, sitting in an auditorium with David Lynch, Robert Altman, Michael Mann, Paul Thomas Anderson, Spike Jonze, and I deserve this win? It's ridiculous. These are my heroes and there am I. Then I thought, 'OK. So I'm going to treat early success in the movies in exactly the same way as I treated early success in the theatre, and work my ass off to prove it was not a fluke. I'm going to earn my spurs, and I'm going to do different movies. I'll make a gangster movie. I'll make a war movie. I'm going to do handheld, I'm going to make family dramas and I'm going to make a big action movie.' And that's what I've done. I didn't work it all out upfront... just that I was going to push, and not make the same movie again, or work in the same style, or repeat myself. That's what I did in the theater, and I made some pretty bad productions in the early years, because I was pushing to see if I was any good at them or if there was some personal connection. Eventually I figured it out by trial and error. I hope it was something important in the making of me."[xlix]

Consider the names Alejandro González Iñárritu, Kathryn Bigelow, James Cameron, or Mel Gibson. Consider the names Miloš Forman, Bob Fosse, or Billy Wilder.[l] Despite all having been handed the Academy Award for Best Director at a point in their lifetime, some of their careers have stretched for decades, while others sporadic. Some were born in the United States, while others came from various parts of the world. Some have kept their work strictly in film, while others have used their talents in other fields. Each made poignant contributions to cinema which have reflected the culture or influenced society. Each of these names influenced lives in one way or another through their artistic creations. Consider the name Sam Mendes and his "bank loan" which clearly has been paid off.

THANK YOU!

The authors and Under One Hour, LLC thank you for your purchase. We truly hope you have found this publication valuable and will check out our other listings on our website here: www.UnderOneHour.com/Books.

We are always looking to hear from our fans so if you liked the book, want to leave a comment, or give some feedback, contact us here: www.UnderOneHour.com/Contact-Us

Please sign up for our newsletter and follow our blog, Facebook, and Twitter to keep updated. We enjoy the interaction through all of these mediums, but feel free to use your favorite one.

If you would like to write your own Under One Hour book, please contact us on our author webpage: www.UnderOneHour.com/Write-For-UOH

Still included in this book are the **Filmography** and **Supplemental Material** with convenient links.

ACKNOWLEDGEMENTS

This book exists because of the extraordinary opportunity offered to me by Andrew Brown, editor and publisher of *Under One Hour, LLC*. Thank you for changing my life. Your series will continue to change other's lives as well.

The unsung hero of this project, editor Claire Tuft whose substantial aid sharpened this book to completion. Claire not only is one of the best editors I've ever worked with, but is also the reason you were able to make sense of anything in this book.

Proper credit is due to Dr. Laurence F. Knapp who educated me not only in film school, but also the proper handling of an academic undertaking such as this. I'm undeserving of such an incredible mentor.

A very special word of gratitude to Ron Falzone, a bona fide expert of all things 007 (and genus of film academia) who helped structure James Bond's historical and cultural significance.

Thank you to film enthusiasts Nick Allen and Eric S. Cunningham, who's professional feedback on various details was invaluable. Additional editing assistance was greatly welcomed thanks to Katie Dorn and Sarah Nadine.

A special shout-out to the staff of Queen of All Saints Basilica who kindly put up with my idiosyncrasies on a daily basis: Rev. Simon Braganza, Rev. Thomas Campana, Rev. Rich Conyers, Kate Dombrowski, Dr. Carole Eipers, Jerry Farrell, Rev. Edward Grace, Pam Hautzinger, Dorothy Kennedy, Mary Morley, Monsignor Wayne Prist, Paul Scavone, Dr. Ken Stoak, and my wonderful employer for nearly a decade, Monsignor John Pollard.

To my family and friends, who's mere existence was tremendous help in ways they probably weren't aware of: Clint Cottrell, the Henik family, Mike Wade Johnson of *Faux Pas Films*, Carleen & Mike Jolls, Tim Jolls, Daniel Jolls, Jennifer Jolls, James Kim, Olia Klein, Karol Matejko, Shon McGregory, Kristine Homan, Steve Lechner and his wife Mariana, Rita Murphy, Robert Murphy, Alla Royfman, Sriram Parthasarathy, Natalia Samoylova, the Solmos family, Monica & Kurt Wachholder, and Bobby Watson.

Finally, endless gratitude to Sam Mendes himself, for sharing his wonderful talent with us.

ABOUT THE AUTHOR

(Director Michael Jolls on the set of *The Great Chicago Filmmaker* with Sriram
Parthasarathy. Photo by Natalia Samoylova.)

Michael Jolls is a producer from Chicago, IL. He adapted historical texts
and articles to bring in screen the documentary *Cathedral of the North Shore*
(2013), a biography of Rev. William Netstreater and his 50-year tenure in the
village of Wilmette, IL. In the interim, Jolls worked as assistant editor on the
book *David Fincher: Interviews* by Dr. Laurence F. Knapp for the University
Press of Mississippi. With long-time collaborator Natalia Samoylova, Jolls
directed *The Great Chicago Filmmaker* (2015), a feature-length mockumentary
showcasing dozens of Chicago-based actors playing themselves in a
fictionalized satire of the independent industry. Jolls has collaborated on
numerous short-films and videos based off the characters co-created with
fellow associates including *6 Rules* (2011); *Uncle Colt & Cletus* (2013); and
#SelfieGuy: A Very Merry Christmas Special (2015).

FILMOGRAPHY

AMERICAN BEAUTY

    DreamWorks Pictures and Jinks/Cohen Company

    Released: September 8th, 1999 (U.S.A.)

    Directed by: **Sam Mendes**

    Written by: Alan Ball

    Produced by: Bruce Cohen, Dan Jinks, Stan Wlodkowski, Alan Ball

    Casting by: Debra Zane

    Director of Photography: Conrad L. Hall

    Edited by: Tariq Anwar and Christopher Greenbury

    Production, Art, and Set Design: Naomi Shohan, David S. Lazan, Jan K. Bergstrom

    Music: Thomas Newman

    Starring: Kevin Spacey, Annette Bening, Thora Birch, Wes Bentley, Mena Suvari, Chris Cooper, Peter Gallagher, Barry Del Sherman, Allison Janney, Scott Bakula, and Sam Robards

    Filming Locations: United States, Great Britain

    Production Budget: $15 million

    Academy Awards: Best Picture, Best Director, Best Actor, Best Original Screenplay, Best Cinematography (won); Best Actress, Best Editing, Best Score (nomination)

    Golden Globe: Best Motion Picture – Drama, Best Director, Best Screenplay (won); Best Actor, Best Actress, Best Score (nomination)

    BAFTA (British Academy of Film and Television Arts): Best Film, Best Actor, Best Actress, Best Cinematography, Best Editing, Best Music (won); Best Direction, Best Supporting Actress, Best Supporting Actress, Best Supporting Actor, Best Original Screenplay, Best Production Design, Best Make-Up, Best Sound (nomination)

    Box Office: $130 million U.S.A. | $356.2 million worldwide

    Running Time: 2 hours and 2 minutes

    MPAA Rating: R for strong sexuality, language, violence, and drug content

ROAD TO PERDITION

DreamWorks Pictures, 20th Century Fox, and Zanuck Company
Released: July 12th, 2002 (U.S.A.)
Directed by: **Sam Mendes**
Written by: David Self (based off the graphic novel by Max Allen
Collins & Richard Piers)
Produced by: **Sam Mendes**, Richard D. Zanuck, Dean Zanuck, Joan
Bradshaw, Tara B. Cook, Cherylanne Martin, and Walter F. Parkes
Casting by: Debra Zane
Director of Photography: Conrad L. Hall
Edited by: Jill Bilcock
Production, Art, and Set Design: Dennis Gassner, Richard L. Johnson,
and Nancy Haigh
Music: Thomas Newman
Starring: Tom Hanks, Paul Newman, Jude Law, Tyler Hoechlin, Daniel
Craig, Jennifer Jason Leigh, Ciarán Hinds, Dylan Baker, Kevin
Chamberlin, Stanley Tucci
Filming Location: United States
Production Budget: $80 million
Academy Awards: Best Cinematography (won); Best Supporting Actor,
Best Art Direction, Best Score, Best Sound, Best Sound Editing
(nomination)
Golden Globe: Best Supporting Actor (nomination)
BAFTA: Best Cinematography, Best Production Design (won); Best
Supporting Actor
Box Office: $104 million U.S.A. | $181 million worldwide
Running Time: 1 hour and 57 minutes
MPAA Rating: R for violence and language

JARHEAD

Universal Pictures, Lucy Fisher/Douglas Wick Productions, and Neal
Street Prdocutions
Released: November 4th, 2005 (U.S.A.)
Directed by: **Sam Mendes**
Written by: William D. Broyles Jr. (based off the book by Anthony
Swofford)
Produced by: Bobby Cohen, Lucy Fisher, Pippa Harris, Douglas Wick,
and Sam Mercer

Casting by: Debra Zane
Director of Photography: Roger Deakins
Edited by: Walter Murch
Production, Art, and Set Design: Dennis Gassner, Stefan Dechant, Marco Niro, Christina Ann Wilson, Nancy Haigh
Music: Thomas Newman
Starring: Jake Gyllenhaal, Peter Sarsgaard, Jamie Foxx, Lucas Black, Evan Jones, Chris Cooper, Martin Papazian
Filming Locations: United States
Production Budget: $70-$72 million
Box Office: $62.6 million U.S.A. | $96.8 million worldwide
Running Time: 2 hours and 5 minutes
MPAA Rating: R for pervasive language, some violent images, and strong sexual content

STARTER FOR 10

BBC Films, HBO Films, Playtone, Scamp Film and Theatre Ltd., and Neal Street Productions
Released: November 10th, 2006 (U.K.)
Directed by: Tom Vaughan
Written by: David Nicholls (based of his novel)
Produced by: Jeff Abberley, Julia Blackman, Diana Choi, Michelle Chydzik Sowa, Gary Goetzman, Tom Hanks, Pippa Harris, Nathalie Marciano, **Sam Mendes**, Mary Richards, Steve Shareshain
Casting by: Nina Gold
Director of Photography: Ashley Rowe
Edited by: Jon Harris & Heather Persons
Production, Art, and Set Design: Sarah Greenwood, Ian Bailie, Nick Gottschalk, Katie Spencer
Music: Blake Neely
Filming Locations: Great Britain
Production Budget: $8.2 million
Starring: James McAvoy, Benedict Cumberbatch, Alice Eve, Rebecca Hall, Dominic Cooper, Catherine Tate, James Corden, Charles Dance
Box Office: $216 thousand U.S.A. | $1.7 million worldwide
Running Time: 1 hour and 36 minutes
MPAA Rating: PG-13 for sexual content, language, and a scene of drug use

THINGS WE LOST IN THE FIRE

DreamWorks Pictures and Neal Street Productions
Released: October 19th, 2007 (U.S.A)
Directed by: Susanne Bier
Written by: Allan Loeb
Produced by: Pippa Harris, Barbara Kelly, Allan Loeb, **Sam Mendes**, Sam Mercer
Casting by: Debra Zane
Director of Photography: Tom Stern
Edited by: Pernille Bech Christenesen, Bruce Cannon
Production, Art, and Set Design: Richard Sherman, Geoff Wallace, Dominique Faquet-Lemaitre
Music: Johan Söderqvist
Starring: Halle Berry, Benicio del Toro, David Duchovny, Alison Lohman, Micah Berry, Alexis Llewellyn, John Carroll Lynch, Omar Benson Miller
Filming Locations: Canada
Production Budget: $16 million
Box Office: $3.2 million U.S.A. | $8.5 million worldwide
Running Time: 1 hour and 58 minutes
MPAA Rating: R for drug content and language

THE KITE RUNNER

DreamWorks Pictures, Sidney Kimmel Entertainment, Participant Productions, and Parkes/MacDonald production
Released: December 14th, 2007 (U.S.A. - limited)
Directed by: Marc Forster
Written by: David Benioff (based off the novel by Khaled Hosseini)
Produced by: William Horberg, Sidney Kimmel, Leslie Lerman, Laurie MacDonald, **Sam Mendes**, Kwame Parker, Walter F. Parks, Jeff Skoll, Bruce Toll, E. Bennett Walsh, Rebecca Teldham
Casting by: Katie Dowd
Director of Photography: Roberto Schaefer
Edited by: Matt Chessé
Production, Art, and Set Design: Carlos Conti, Karen Murphy, Maria Nay, and Caroline Smith
Music: Alberto Iglesias

Starring: Khalid Abdalla, Atossa Leoni, Shawn Toub, Zekeria Ebrahimi, Ahmad Khan Mahmoodzada, Homayoun Ershadi, Nasser Memarzia
Filming Locations: Afghanistan, China, United States
Production Budget: $20 million
Academy Awards: Best Score (nomination)
Golden Globe: Best Foreign Language Film, Best Score (nomination)
BAFTA: Best Adapted Screenplay, Best Foreign Language Film, Best Music (nomination)
Box Office: $15.8 million U.S.A. | $73.2 million worldwide
Running Time: 2 hours and 8 minutes
MPAA Rating: PG-13 for strong thematic material including rape of a child, violence, and brief strong language

REVOLUTIONARY ROAD

DreamWorks Pictures, BBC Films, Evamere Entertainment, and Neal Street Productions
Released: December 26th 2008 (limited) | January 23rd, 2009 (wide, U.S.A.)
Directed by: **Sam Mendes**
Written by: Justin Haythe (based off the novel by Richard Yates)
Produced by: Gina Amoroso, Bobby Cohen, Henry Fernaine, Pippa Harris, John N. Hart, Peter Kalmbach, **Sam Mendes**, Marion Rosenberg, Ann Ruark, Scott Rudin, David M. Thompson, Nina Wolarsky
Casting by: Ellen Lewis and Debra Zane
Director of Photography: Roger Deakins
Edited by: Tariq Anwar
Production, Art, and Set Design: Teresa Carriher-Thayer, John Kasarda, Nicholas Lundy, Debra Schutt, and Kristi Zea
Music: Thomas Newman
Starring: Leonardo DiCaprio, Kate Winslet, Kathy Bates, Richard Easton, David Harbour, Kathryn Hahn, Zoe Kazan, Ryan Simpkins, Ty Simpkins, Michael Shannon, Dylan Baker
Filming Locations: United States
Production Budget: $35 million
Academy Awards: Best Supporting Actor, Best Art Direction, Best Costume (nomination)
Golden Globe: Best Actress (won); Best Motion Picture, Best Director, Best Actor (nomination)

BAFTA: Best Adapted Screenplay, Best Actress, Best Production
Design, Best Costume (nomination)
Box Office: $22.9 million U.S.A. | $75.2 million worldwide
Running Time: 1 hour and 59 minutes
MPAA Rating: R for language and some sexual content/nudity

AWAY WE GO

Focus Features, Big Beach/Edward Saxon Productions, and Neal Street
Productions
Released: June 5th, 2009 (limited, U.S.A.)
Directed by: **Sam Mendes**
Written by: Dave Eggers & Vendela Vida
Produced by: Pippa Harris, Peter Sarah, Edward Saxon, Marc
Turtletaub, Corinne Golden Weber, Mari-Joe Winkler
Casting by: Ellen Lewis and Debra Zane
Director of Photography: Ellen Kuras
Edited by: Sarah Flack
Production, Art, and Set Design: Jess Gonchor, Henry Dunn, Lydia
Marks
Music: Alexi Murdoch
Starring: John Krasinski, Maya Rudolph, Catherine O'Hara, Jeff Daniels,
Allison Janney, Jim Gaffigan, Carmen Ejogo, Maggie Gyllenhaal, Josh
Hamilton, Chris Messina, Melanie Lynskey, Paul Schneider
Filming Locations: United States
Production Budget: $17 million
Box Office: $9.4 million U.S.A. | $14.8 million worldwide
Running Time: 1 hour and 38 minutes
MPAA Rating: R for language and some sexual content

OUT OF THE ASHES

Bungalow Town Productions, Shabash Productions
Released: October 29th, 2010 (U.K.)
Directed by: Tim Albone, Lucy Martens
Co-Director: Leslie Knott
Produced by: Tim Albone, Leslie Knott, **Sam Mendes**, Tom Roberts,
Greg Sanderson, Rachel Wexler
Director of Photography: Tim Albone, Lucy Martens
Edited by: Gregor Lyon

Music: Andrew Phillips
Starring: Hasti Gul Abid, Taj Malik Aleem, Geoffrey Boycott, Kabir
Khan, Nawruz, Gulbudeen Naib, Karim Sediq, Ahmed Shah
Running Time: 1 hour and 26 minutes

THE HOLLOW CROWN

Neal Street Productions, NBC Universal Television, WNET Thirteen,
BBC
Released: June 30th, 2012 / May 7th, 2016
Seasons: 2012 and 2016
Directed by: Dominic Cooke, Richard Eyre, Rupert Goold, Thea
Sharrock
Written by: Ben Power, William Shakespeare, Richard Eyre, Rupert
Goold, Thea Sharrock
Produced by: Pippa Harris, **Sam Mendes**, Gareth Neame, Rupert Ryle-
Hodges, David Horn, Nicola Brown, Angie Daniell
Casting by: Maggie Lunn, Sam Jones
Director of Photography: Ben Smithard, Zac Nicholson, Danny Cohen,
Michael McDonough
Edited by: Gareth C. Scales, Trevow Waite, Lesley Walker, John Wilson
Music by: Dan Jones, Stephen Warbeck, Adam Cork, Adrian Johnston
Starring: Tom Hiddleston, Benedict Cumberbatch, Tom Hughes, Ben
Whishaw, Simon Russell Beale, Michelle Dockery, Clémence Poésy,
Jeremy Irons, Michael Gambon, Patrick Stewart, Julie Walters, Keeley
Hawes, John Hurt
Filming Locations: United Kingdom
BAFTA: Best Actor, Best Original Television Music, Best Supporting
Actor (won); Best Single Drama, Best Costume Design

SKYFALL

Eon Productions, B23, Twentieth Century Fox, Sony Pictures, Metro-
Goldwyn-Mayer
Released: October 26th, 2012 (U.K.)
Directed by: **Sam Mendes**
Written by: Neal Purvis, Robert Wade, and John Logan (based off the
characters created by Ian Fleming)
Produced by: Barbara Broccoli, Chiu Wah Lee, Callum McDougall,
Andrew Noakes, David Pope, Gregg Wilson, Michael G. Wilson

Casting by: Debbie McWilliams
Director of Photography: Roger Deakins
Edited by: Stuart Baird
Production, Art, and Set Design: Dennis Gassner, Neal Callow, Dean Clegg, James Foster, Mark Harris, Marc Homes, Paul Inglis, Jason Knox-Johnston, Chris Lowe, Anna Pinnock
Music: Thomas Newman
Starring: Daniel Craig, Judi Dench, Javier Bardem, Ralph Fiennes, Naomie Harris, Bérénice Marloe, Albert Finney, Ben Whishaw, Rory Kimmear, Ola Rapace
Filming Locations: Great Britain, Japan, Turkey
Production Budget: $200 million
Academy Awards: Best Original Song, Best Sound Editing (won); Best Cinematography, Best Score, Best Sound Mixing (nomination)
Golden Globe: Best Original Song (won)
BAFTA: Best British Film, Best Music (won); Best Supporting Actor, Best Supporting Actress, Best Cinematography, Best Editing, Best Production Design, Best Sound (nomination)
Box Office: $304.3 million U.S.A. | $1.1 billion worldwide
Running Time: 2 hours and 23 minutes
MPAA Rating: PG-13 for intense violent sequences throughout, some sexuality, language, and smoking

BLOOD

Neal Street Productions
Released: May 31st, 2013 (U.K.)
Directed by: Nick Murphy
Written by: Bill Gallagher (based off his miniseries)
Produced by: James Atherton, Andrew Critchley, Stuart Ford, Peter Hampden, Pippa Harris, Lee Hodgkinson, Christine Langan, Nick Laws, **Sam Mendes**, Norman Merry, Jan Pace, Michael Roban, Nicola Shindler
Casting by: Nina Gold
Director of Photography: George Richmond
Edited by: Victoria Boydell
Production, Art, and Set Design: Cristina Casali, Pawlow Wintoniuk, Anita Gupta
Music: Daniel Pemberton

Starring: Paul Bettany, Stephen Graham, Brian Cox, Mark Strong, Ben Crompton, Naomi Battrik, Zoë Tapper, Natasha Little
Running Time: 1 hour and 32 minutes
MPAA Rating: Not Rated

PENNY DREADFUL

Neal Street Productions, Desert Wolf Productions
Released: April 28th, 2014 (internet)
Seasons: 2014, 2015, 2016
Directed by: James Hawes, Brian Kirk, Paco Cabezas, J.A. Bayona, Coky Giedroyc, Dearbhla Walsh, Damon Thomas, Kari Skogland
Written by: John Logan
Produced by: Pippa Harris, Sheila Hockin, Chris W. King, John Logan, **Sam Mendes**, Nicholas Brown, James Flynn, Morgan O'Sullivan, Karen Richards, Nicolás Tapia, Belén Atenza
Casting by: Karen Lindsay-Stewart, Frank Moiselle, Nuala Moiselle
Director of Photography: John Conroy, Owen McPolin, P.J. Dillon, Nigel Willoughby, Xavi Giménez
Edited by: Christopher Donaldson, Michele Conroy, Aaron Marshall, Geoff Ashenhurst, Jaume Martí, Bernat Vilaplana, Gareth C. Scales
Production, Art, and Set Design by: Jonathan McKinstry, Jo Riddell, Antonio Calvo-Dominguez, John King, Gary McGinty, Shane McEnroe, Colman Corish, Conor Dennison, Adam O'Neill, Anais Chareyre, Philip Murphy, Damian Byrne
Music: Abel Korzeniowski
Starring: Reeve Carney, Timothy Dalton, Eva Green, Rory Kinnear, Billie Piper, Harry Treadaway, Josh Hartnett, Danny Sapani, Simon Russell Beate, Douglas Hodge, Sarah Greene
Filming Locations: Ireland, Spain
Emmy Award(s): Outstanding Make-Up, Outstanding Title Music, Outstanding Score (nomination)
Golden Globe(s): Best Actress (nomination)
BAFTA(s): Best Production Design, Best Music, Best Make-Up (won); Best Make-Up (nomination)
Running Time: Each episode approximately 1 hour

SPECTRE

    Eon Productions, B24, Sony Pictures, Columbia Pictures, Danjaq, Metro-Goldwyn-Mayer

    Released: October 26th, 2015 (U.K.)

    Directed by: **Sam Mendes**

    Written by: John Logan, Neal Purvis, Robert Wade, and Jez Butterworth (based off the characters created by Ian Fleming)

    Produced by: Zakaria Alaoui, Barbara Broccoli, Daniel Craig, Robert Malerba, Callum McDougall, Andrew Noakes, Stacy Perskie, David Pope, Wolfgang Rammi, Jayne-Ann Tenggren, Gregg Wilson, Michael G. Wilson

    Casting by: Debbie McWilliams

    Director of Photography: Hoyte Van Hoytema

    Edited by: Lee Smith

    Production, Art, and Set Design: Dennis Gassner, Andrew Bennett, Neal Callow, Dean Clegg, Ben Collins, Mark Harris, Chris Lowe, Anna Pinnock

    Music: Thomas Newman

    Starring: Daniel Craig, Christoph Waltz, Léa Seydoux, Ralph Fiennes, Monica Bellucci, Ben Whishaw, Naomie Harris, Dave Bautista, Andrew Scott, Rory Kinnear, Jesper Christensen

    Filming Locations: Austria, Great Britain, Italy, Mexico, Morocco

    Production Budget: $245 million

    Academy Awards: Best Original Song (won)

    Golden Globe: Best Original Song (won)

    Box Office: $200 million U.S.A. | $880.6 million worldwide

    Running Time: 2 hours and 28 minutes

    MPAA Rating: PG-13 for intense sequences of action and violence, some disturbing images, sensuality, and language

THE VOYEUR'S MOTEL

    Amblin Entertainment, DreamWorks Pictures, Neal Street Productions

    Released: 2018

    Directed by: **Sam Mendes**

    Written by: Krysty Wilson-Cairns (based off the novel by Gay Talese)

    Produced by: Pippa Harris, **Sam Mendes**, and Steven Spielberg

SUPPLEMENTAL MATERIAL

SAM MENDES INTERVIEWS

➤ Joshua Klein, "American Beauty."
    The AV Club, September 29th, 1999.
➤ Simon Fanshawe, "Sam Smiles."
    The Guardian, January 22nd, 2000.
➤ Andrew L. Urban, "Sam Mendes: American Beauty."
    Urban Cinefile, February 2000.
➤ Jeff Gordcuer, "Oscar Preview: American Beauty."
    Entertainment Weekly, March 200.
➤ Time Magazine, "A Private, Interior Film."
    Time Asia, Spring 2000.
➤ Paul Fisher, "Tom Hanks, Road to Perdition interview."
    Cranky Critic: Star Talk, July 2002.
➤ Kevin Jackson, "Anatomy of Murder."
    Sight and Sound, September 2002.
➤ Simon Braund, "The Killer Elite."
    Empire, September 2002.
➤ Judy Sloane, "The Road to the Oscars."
    Film Review, October 2002.
➤ Empire Magazine Staff, "54 Films for Your Consideration."
    Empire, November 2005.
➤ Rob Carnevale, "Jarhead – Sam Mendes Interview."
    indieLondon, Fall 2005.
➤ Author Unlisted, "Sam Mendes and Jake Gyllenhaal on 'Jarhead'."
    Film4, Date Unspecified.
➤ Scott Bowles, "War is the Workplace in Jarhead."
    USA Today, October 31st, 2005.
➤ Jacki Lyden, "'Jarhead' and the Attraction of War."
    NPR, All Things Considered, (Radio Transcript), November 5th, 2005.
➤ Andrew Graham-Dixon, "Interview with Sam Mendes."
    The Telegraph/BBC's The Culture Show, December 11th, 2005.
➤ Matt Mueller, "American Beauty."
    Total Film, October 2008.

- NYC Movie Guru, "Interview with Leonardo DiCaprio, Kate Winslet, Kathy Bates, Michael Shannon, stars, and Sam Mendes, director of Revolutionary Road."
  The NYC Movie Guru, December 2008.
- Gaby Wood, "How Sam Became the Man."
  The Guardian, December 13th, 2008.
- Dan Jolin, "2009 Oscars: Kate Winslet & Revolutionary Road."
  Empire, January 2009.
- Richard K. Bosley, "Close Focus."
  American Cinematographer, January 2009.
- Unlisted, "Revolutionary Road: Sam Mendes interview."
  Cinema.com, Winter 2008
- Scott Tobias, "Sam Mendes Interview."
  The A.V. Club, June 2nd, 2009.
- Alex Simon, "Sam Mendes Hits the Road in 'Away We Go'."
  The Hollywood Interview, June 14th, 2009.
- Dave Calhoun, "Sam Mendes Interview."
  Time Out London, Fall 2012.
- Dan Jolin, "We've Been Expecting You Mr. Bond."
  Empire, October 2012.
- Mark Salisbury, "James Bond: Secrets from the set of Skyfall."
  The Telegraph, October 16th, 2012.
- Frank Lovece, "Skyfall Rising."
  Film Journal, November 2012.
- Luke Y. Thompson, "Interview: Sam Mende's Revolutionary Road to directing James Bond."
  Nerdist, November 1st, 2012.
- Drew Taylor, "Interview: Sam Mendes."
  IndieWire, November 6th, 2012.
- Mark Hope-Jones, "MI6 Under Siege."
  American Cinematographer, December 2012.
- Kate Kellaway, "Sam Mendes: 'I did Skyfall to wake myself up. It has certainly done that."
  The Guardian, December 8th, 2012.
- Chris Tilly, "Sam Mendes Lists His Movie Inspirations."
  IGN, March 25th, 2013.
- Charlie Schmidlin, "Sam Mendes says he felt 'Physically Ill at Prospect of 'Skyfall' sequel."
  IndieWire/The Playlist, April 26th, 2013.
- Michael Gioia, "Playbill Exclusive: Interview with director Sam Mendes."
  Roundabout Theatre Company, March 20th, 2014.

- ➢ Bruce Handy, "Sam Mendes on Bringing Mature 'Bond Girls' to Spectre."
  Vanity Fair, October 27th, 2015.
- ➢ Simon Brew, "Spectre: Sam Mendes on the difficulties of the opening scene."
  Den of Geek, October 27th, 2015.
- ➢ Chris Lee, "Spectre of Death."
  Entertainment Weekly, October 30th, 2015.
- ➢ Sam Mendes, "Auteur Theories."
  Empire, November, 2015.
- ➢ Chris Hewitt, "We Just Push Each Other."
  Empire, November, 2015.
- ➢ Adam Smith, "Look Closer."
  Empire, November, 2015.
- ➢ Mike Fleming Jr., "His Exit Interview?"
  Deadline Hollywood, November 5th, 2015.
- ➢ Demetrious Mateou, "Sam Mendes Talks Bond, American Beauty, and Film vs. Theatre at BAFTA."
  IndieWire, December 23rd, 2015.

ADDITIONAL INTERVIEWS

- ➢ Adam Smith, "Top Cat."
  Empire, February, 2000.
- ➢ Paul Fischer, "Tom Hanks, Road to Perdition interview."
  Cranky Critic, July, 2002.
- ➢ Krista Smith, "Isn't She Deneuvely?"
  Vanity Fair, December 2008.
- ➢ Karen Valby, "The Unsinkable Kate and Leo."
  Entertainment Weekly, December 18th, 2008.
- ➢ Susan Wloszczyna, "A Revolutionary Road for Titanic friends."
  USA Today, December 23rd, 2008.
- ➢ Susan King, "Michael Shannon's 'Revolutionary Road'".
  Los Angeles Times, January 9, 2009.
- ➢ Stella Papamichael, "Revolutionary Road: Leonardo DiCaprio interview."
  BBC, January 28th, 2009.
- ➢ Julie Weiner, "Bond Ambition."
  Vanity Fair, November, 2012.
- ➢ Leah Curtus, "In Depth: Thomas Newman."

Beyond Cinema, Winter 2012.

➢ Simon Baines, "Thomas Newman: The Man Behind the Soundtracks to *American Beauty*, *Spectre*, and More."
Theversion.co.uk, October 16th, 2015.

➢ Alex Dilmes, "Daniel Craig is Esquire's October Cover Star."
Esquire, October 21, 2015.

➢ Chris Hewitt, "The Phantom Menace."
Empire, November, 2015.

➢ Dan Powell, "Spectre - Dave Bautista Q and A."
What Culture, February, 2016.

➢ Marianne Zumberge, "Sam Smith reveals what goes into a classic Bond theme."
Variety, February 25, 2016.

CRITICAL AND ANALYTICAL ARTICLES

➢ Ted Slafsky, Joannie M. Schrof, Stephen J. Hedges, Richard Z. Chesnoff, Peter Cary, Louise Lief, Brain Duffy, "The World's Most Dangerous Man."
U.S. News and World Report, June 4th, 1990.

➢ Arthur Chu, "Complaining Like It's 1999."
The Daily Beast, June 3rd, 2014.

➢ Andrew Pulver, "Making A Killing: Why James Bond is Forever."
The Guardian, December 5th, 2014.

➢ Zack Sharf, "The Film of Sam Mendes, ranked from worse to best."
IndieWire, February 6th, 2015.

➢ Kyle Anderson, "James Bond at 53"
The '60s, October 10th, 2015
The '70s, October 16th, 2015
The '80s, October 23rd, 2015
The '90s (and One Extra), October 31st, 2015
The Daniel Craig Years, November 7th, 2015
The Nerdist

BOOKS

➢ Alan Ball. American Beauty: The Shooting Script, 1999.
➢ Matt Wolf. Sam Mendes at the Donmar: Stepping into Freedom, 2002.

ENDNOTES

[i] Steven Spielberg for *Schindler's List* in 1993. Clint Eastwood for *Unforgiven* in 1992. Ron Howard for *A Beautiful Mind* in 2001. Martin Scorsese for *The Departed* in 2006. Each of these films would also win Best Picture.

[ii] Christopher Nolan with *Batman Begins* (2005); *The Dark Knight* (2008); *Inception* (2010); *The Dark Knight Rises* (2012); and *Interstellar* (2014). Tim Burton with *Batman* (1989); *Batman Returns* (1992); *Sleepy Hollow* (1999); *Planet of the Apes* (2001); *Charlie and the Chocolate Factory* (2005); and *Alice in Wonderland* (2010). Darren Aronofsky with *Black Swan* (2010) and *Noah* (2014). Nancy Meyers with *Something's Gotta Give* (2003) and *It's Complicated* (2009). David Fincher with *Se7en* (1995); *The Curious Case of Benjamin Button* (2008); *The Girl with the Dragon Tattoo* (2011); and *Gone Girl* (2014). Paul Greengrass with *The Bourne Supremacy* (2004); *The Bourne Ultimatum* (2007); *Captain Phillips* (2013); and *Jason Bourne* (2016).

[iii] David Poland, "DP/30: *Spectre*, Sam Mendes". *DP/30 The Oral History of Hollywood*. November 7, 2015.

[iv] *The Killing* (1956); *Paths of Glory* (1957); *Spartacus* (1960); and *Lolita* (1962). Both *Paths of Glory* and *Spartacus* were added to The Criterion Collection.

[v] Simon Fanshaw, "Sam Smiles", *The Guardian* (January 22, 2000).

[vi] Alex Simon, "Sam Mendes Hits the Road with *Away We Go*", *The Hollywood Interview* (June 14, 2009).

[vii] Mike Fleming Jr., "His Exit Interview? *Spectre*'s Sam Mendes on his role in the transformation of James Bond", *Deadline Hollywood* (November 5, 2015).

[viii] David Poland, "DP/30 *Spectre*, Sam Mendes" *DP/30: The Oral History of Hollywood*, (November 6, 2015).

[ix] Susan Wloszczyna, "A Revolutionary Road to Titanic friends", *U.S.A. Today* (December 23, 2008).

[x] Judy Sloane, "The Road to the Oscars", *Film Review* (October 2002).

[xi] Gaby Wood, "How Sam Became The Man", *The Guardian* (December 13, 2008).

[xii] Ibid, x.

[xiii] Audio- Commentary, 1999.

[xiv] Andrew L. Urban, "Sam Mendes: *American Beauty*," *Urban Cinefile* (February 2000).

[xv] Time, "A Private, Interior Film", TIME Asia (Spring 2000).

[xvi] Joshua Klein, *"American Beauty"*, *The Onion/The AV Club* (September 29th, 1999).

[xvii] Ibid, xiv.

[xviii] Demetrious Matheou, "Sam Mendes talks Bond, *American Beauty*, and Film vs. Theatre at BAFTA", *IndieWire* (December 3rd, 2015).

[xix] Simon Braud, "The Killer Elite". *Empire*, September 2002.

[xx] *Spider-Man* earned $114.8 million in its opening weekend, making it the highest grossing opening ever; it would hold that record for four years until being surpassed by *Pirates of the Caribbean: Dead Man's Chest* (2006, Gore Verbinski) with $135.6 million. *Spider-Man* was the highest grossing film of 2002, earning $403.7 million domestically and $418 million in foreign markets, a total of $821.7 million worldwide.

[xxi] Audio-commentary, 2002.

[xxii] Ibid, xxi.

[xxiii] The book details the Rooney family controlling three cities; two in west Illinois, and one in Iowa.

[xxiv] Simon Baines, "Thomas Newman – The Man Behind the Soundtracks to *Spectre*, *American Beauty*, and More". *theversion.co.uk*, October 16, 2015.

[xxv] Author Unlisted, "Color, Melody and… Perfume", *Motion Picture Editors Guild Newsletter*, January/February, 1996.

[xxvi] Ibid, xxi.

[xxvii] Dan Jolin, "2009 Oscars: Kate Winslet and *Revolutionary Road*," *Empire* (January 2009).

[xxviii] Ted Slafsky, Joannie M. Schrof, Stephen J. Hedges, Richard Z. Chesnoff, Peter Cary, Louise Lief, Brian Duffy, "The World's Most Dangerous Man," *U.S. News & World Report* (June 4, 1990).

[xxix] Scott Bowles, "War is the Workplace in *Jarhead* (October 31, 2005).

[xxx] With the exception of various documentaries and the 9/11 films *United 93* (2006, Paul Greengrass) and *World Trade Center* (2006, Oliver Stone) virtually all big-budgeted productions about the wars in Afghanistan and Iraq were fictional stories, albeit some loosely based off of real events: *Home of the Brave* (2006, Irwin Winkler); *Grace is Gone* (2007, James C. Strouse); *The Kingdom* (2007, Peter Berg); *Lions for Lambs* (2007, Robert Redfrod); *Redacted* (2007, Brian De Palma); *In the Valley of Elah* (2007, Paul Haggis); *Body of Lies* (2008, Ridley Scott); *Stop-Loss* (2008, Kimberly Peirce); *Brothers* (2009, Jim

Sheridan); *The Hurt Locker* (2009, Kathryn Bigelow); *The Messenger* (2009, Oren Moverman); and *Green Zone* (2010, Paul Greengrass)

xxxi After Usama bin Laden's assassination on May 1st, 2011, the war-on-terror genre drastically changed. *Zero Dark Thirty* (2012, Kathryn Bigelow) which depicted the famous assassination, was the first in the genre that depicted a true story. *Zero Dark Thirty*, which released at very end of 2012 and advanced to wide release in early 2013, became the most financially successful of the war-on-terror genre, earning $95.7 million in the U.S. domestic box office. One year later, *Lone Survivor* (2013, Peter Berg) based off a best-selling memoir by Navy SEAL Marcus Luttrell recounting his experience in Afghanistan, was released during the winter season and earned $125 million in the U.S. domestic box office. The following year, again, another memoir by Navy SEAL Chris Kyle would release, however *American Sniper* (2014, Clint Eastwood) would not only become the top-grossing film of 2014 with $350.1 million domestically and an additional $197.3 million in foreign markets, but became the most controversial film in the genre. Additional films based on true events surrounding terrorism would continue to release throughout the 2010's including *Truth* (2015, James Vanderbilt); *13 Hours: The Secret Soldiers of Benghazi* (2016, Michael Bay); *Whiskey Tango Foxtrot* (2016, Glenn Ficarra & John Requa); *War Dogs* (2016, Todd Phillips); and *Patriot's Day* (2016, Peter Berg).

xxxii Audio-commentary, Sam Mendes, 2005.

xxxiii Andrew Graham-Dixon, "Interview with Sam Mendes," *The Telegraph/BBC's The Culture Show*, (December 11, 2005).

xxxiv Ibid, xxxiii.

xxxv Ibid, xxxiii.

xxxvi Ibid, xxix.

xxxvii Both films are based off books. *Letters from Iwo Jima* screenplay was written by Iris Yamashita and Paul Haggis based off the book *Picture Letters from Commander and Chief* by Tadamichi Kuribayashi, edited by Eric Searleman. *Flags of our Fathers'* screenplay was written by William Broyles Jr. and Paul Haggis; the book was written by James Bradley with Ron Powers.

xxxviii Adam Quigley, "Darren Aronofsky's The Wrestler and Black Swan Started as One Movie", Film Blogging in The Real World. August 31, 2010.

xxxix Richard Lacayo, "All Time 100 Novels". *TIME*, January 6, 2010.

xl Audio-commentary, 2009.

xli Sam Mendes, "Lives of Quiet Desperation: The Making of Revolutionary Road". Blu-ray. 2008.

xlii Kyle Anderson, "James Bond at 53: The 70's", *The Nerdist*, October 16, 2015.

xliii Kyle Anderson, "James Bond at 53: The 80's" *The Nerdist*, October 23, 2015.

xliv Audio-commentary, 2004.

xlv *The Bourne Ultimatum* earned $227.4 million domestically, a total of $442.8 million worldwide. The film won BAFTA awards for Best Editing and Best Sound, while also being nominated for Best British Film, Best Director, Cinematography, and Best Visual Effects. It would win all its Academy Award nominations: Best Editing, Best Sound Mixing, and Best Sound Editing.

The Dark Knight earned $534.5 million domestically, totaling over $1 billion worldwide. It would win a BAFTA award for Best Supporting Actor, with nominations in Best Cinematography, Best Film Editing, Best Production Design, Best Costume Design, Best Film Music, Best Sound, Best Visual Effects, Best Makeup & Hair. It won a Golden Globe Award for Best Supporting Actor. It won two Academy Awards for Best Supporting Actor and Best Sound Editing, while also earning nominations for Best Cinematography, Best Editing, Best Art Direction, Best Makeup, Best Sound Mixing, and Best Visual Effects.

xlvi Daniel Craig, "Becoming Bond," 2006.

xlvii Drew Taylor, "Interview: Sam Mendes," *IndieWire*, November 6, 2012.

xlviii Audio-commentary, 2012.

xlix Mike Fleming Jr., "His Exit Interview? *Spectre*'s Sam Mendes on his role in the transformation of James Bond," *Deadline Hollywood*. November 5th, 2015.

l Alejandro González Iñárritu for *The Revenant* in 2015, and *Birdman* in 2014. He was born in Mexico. Kathryn Bigelow for *The Hurt Locker* in 2009. Her career has been on/off for years since the late 1980s. James Cameron for *Titanic* in 1997. He was born in Canada, and has spent a number of years working with National Geographic on deep-sea dives and archological studies. Mel Gibson for *Braveheart* in 1995. The the majority of his film work has been as an actor. Miloš Forman for *Amadeus* in 1984, and *One Flew Over the Cuckoo's Nest* in 1975. He was born in Czechoslovakia. Bob Fosse for *Cabaret* in 1972. He spent the majority of his career as a musical theatre choreographer. Billy Wilder for *The Apartment* in 1960, and *The Lost Weekend* in 1945. He was born in Austria and survived Nazi-German with many family members killed in the holocaust. Three of Wilder's Oscars were for his screenplays. Bob Fosse and Billy Wilder are two of the biggest director influences on Sam Mendes.

36097822R00063

Made in the USA
Middletown, DE
24 October 2016